Finding God in a Season of Caregiving

FINDING STRENGTH IN A SEASON OF CAREGIVING

100 Days of Devotions for Caregivers

BY:

RICHARD D. CROOKS

The Lord God is my strength, and He has made my feet like hinds' feet, and makes me walk on my high places.

---Habakkuk 3:19

Finding God in a Season of Caregiving

I WOULD LIKE TO DEDICATE THIS BOOK TO THE MEMORY OF THE ONES I WAS CARING FOR WHEN I LEARNED MANY OF THE LESSONS SHARED IN THESE PAGES--NADINE AND LEON CROOKS, MY PARENTS. THE PICTURE WAS ONE I TOOK OF THEM AS WE CELEBRATED THEIR 50TH ANNIVERSARY IN WASHINGTON. THEY DID NOT GET TO SEE THIS BOOK PUBLISHED, THOUGH DAD KNEW IT WAS IN THE WORKS. I WOULD SAY THAT THEY MIGHT SEE IT FROM HEAVEN, BUT I SUSPECT THERE ARE BETTER THINGS TO DO THERE THAN LOOK DOWN AT A BOOK HERE ON EARTH.

--RICHARD CROOKS, 2014

Finding God in a Season of Caregiving

TABLE OF CONTENTS

Finding God in a Season of Caregiving

LETTER TO MY READERS

Dear Reader,

It was my privilege to help care for my parents over the last four and a half years. For about a decade they needed my help in various ways, and to provide that help required many long distance trips on my part, until my wife and I decided to move to my hometown to assist them. There have been many things that were totally unexpected and could not have been predicted, things like how hard it was to keep Dad encouraged as Mom's illness progressed, or how much he depended on my advice for some of the simplest tasks. Sharing that time resulted in a special bond I had with them for the final years of their lives. Some of them brought hardship into their lives, and to a lesser extent, into mine. But it was a good experience, an experience that came to its close during the writing of this book. The pages that follow reflect that experience and my own love of scripture. It is my hope that they will bring something special to your experience and enhance your love of scripture as well.

If you are a caregiver, there is a fair chance that you are "alone" in the company of millions! That is, the responsibilities you carry are similar to those carried by many others in our world. But those others are caring for other people in other places. You are the one doing the work of caring support in your situation. It is a very noble, but challenging life to live. And caregiving is a task that does not receive great notoriety in our American culture. Yet, it is one of the most significant things you will ever do in your life. And it is a calling that is near to the heart of God, because it is the essence of love itself.

It is also one of the most difficult and heart wrenching tasks one can do, too. There is never enough time. You are never able to accomplish some of the things you wish *you could accomplish. Some of the things you observe break your heart. Some of the decisions you are called upon to make are some of the hardest decisions of your life. And all of those things take a toll on you.*

But it is also one of the most rewarding undertakings a person can experience. Even with some of the more simple tasks you do, you are doing something that really does make a difference in the life of another person. And during the times when the responsibility seems too large and God seems far away, when you begin to feel all alone and helpless, I invite you to come to these pages and share a bit of my world, so that you may know that there are others who have been where you are and who would advise you that what you are doing is powerfully special.

There is not a specific sequential order to the devotions (though the structure is not totally random, either) so feel free to jump around in whatever order you think might be most helpful for your own needs. Especially in that case, you may find the indices and appendices useful.

Finally, I would be remiss to not express my appreciation to those friends and family members whose encouragement and support made these pages possible, and especially to those who so generously offered invaluable feedback and suggestions on the materials you are holding. A special thanks to my editing partners, Glenn Machlan and Sandy Sherry, and to my long term friend, Lewis Hevel, who with my wife posed for the cover photo. Most of all, I would express my heartfelt thanks to my wife, Nola, for her willingness to join me in what has been a rewarding and challenging venture of caregiving, and then writing about it. Thank you, one and all.

God bless you in your ministry of caregiving,
Richard

Each week will begin with a special prayer for you. Absorb it, receive the answer, reflect on it whenever you need some courage, and remember: odds are I am not the only person praying for you.

MY PRAYER FOR YOU THIS WEEK

My prayer for you this week is that you will have a truly sound mind. In every decision you make this week, may God's wisdom guide your choices. As you handle the necessary details of daily living, may your thoughts be clear and your planning successful. And may God ease the cares that turn into worries, transforming them all into trust. Amen.

Day 1 Genesis 22:1-8

There are lots of stories in the Bible about families spending time together. Some are not so happy, like the time Cain and Abel went to the field and Cain killed his brother. Others are pretty special, like the time Jacob saw the love of his life for the first time, Rachel, at the well.

In Abraham's old age, he ascended a hill with his son, Isaac, to offer Isaac up as a sacrifice. This story is a very touching and mysterious one. Perhaps you remember it, but if not, one day when you have enough time, take time to read the whole thing. It is one of the most well-known and beloved stories in the Bible. Neither of them knew exactly what was ahead as they walked that path together. On that day, Abraham and Isaac had an unusual experience, a life changing event that neither of them would ever forget.

Life is always unpredictable, and shorter than many of us realize. During this time of caregiving, I want to challenge you to find a way to intentionally make some special memories with your loved one. The opportunities you have may be very limited in time or in scope, so you may think they aren't worth the bother, but don't neglect them; they are opportunities nonetheless. Like Abraham and Isaac, they may be life changing moments, resulting in good stories to pass along to future generations.

One of the great satisfactions I have had is knowing that my efforts have helped to make the declining years of my parents' lives just a little bit better, with the result that I have inherited some pretty special memories. Sometimes the memories are simple things, like the time we bought a live lobster to have for Independence Day...in *Kansas*! Some involved special planning, like anniversary receptions or memorable trips to favorite places. Now that they are gone, those memories are very precious. In the midst of it all, it is hard not to get overburdened or all entangled with the load of caregiving. But it is kind of a "seeing the forest for the trees" sort of thing...make sure you include times of special meanings in the midst of the challenging tasks.

Day 2 Luke 22:39-46

The end of life for Jesus was certainly not easy, was it? Most of us don't experience the kind of traumatic earthly end that He faced. I can't imagine what it would be like, and hope I never know. Even *He* wrestled with what He knew was ahead, and asked God if there were any other alternatives. Then, when He knew He must go forward, in His agony of prayer as He sweated great drops like blood, He experienced an angel coming to Him to give Him the strength He would need.

Nobody ever told us it was going to be easy. When I first decided to move into the caregiving role, I don't know what I really expected it to be. But I know I didn't realize it would be as difficult, time consuming or long as it has turned out to be. I have no regrets at the choice made, even though much was not as I anticipated. But I believe

6

that I have been following God's leading, which is something that really helps in the struggling times.

I think Jesus also had no regrets over His choice, and did what He did because He knew that the Father's will is always, indeed, the best. I guess it just helps to know that I'm not the only one who has struggled in difficult times. You aren't, either. Jesus understands our struggle. He's been there, too. And He is willing to share the strength that helped Him get through it all, so that you can come through victorious as well. As He so pointedly demonstrated for the disciples, admonishing them to follow the example, remember this: prayer is the key.

Day 3 Hebrews 4:15-16

Some days for caregivers are such that you can feel very isolated, and believe that absolutely nobody understands. Then you run across verses like these, and discover that there IS somebody Who understands: your High Priest, Jesus. He understands. He knows what it is like to have so many demands placed upon your time that you cannot possibly meet them all. He knows what it is like to not be able to be everywhere people think you need to be, and to try to juggle everybody's demands and expectations while pursuing the things you know are what you need to be doing.

In theological discussions, there is an interesting balance concerning ideas called the transcendence and the immanence of God. Big words. But even bigger ideas. With powerful meaning for us as we deal with life's demands.

The teachings about the transcendence of God remind us how far beyond our understanding and experience the fullness of God truly is. We cannot even begin to comprehend all that God is, or imagine the vastness of His power (or love or wisdom or anything else about God). At the same time, God chooses not to dwell in aloofness far from us, but to come near to us, as near as our next breath. This is most clearly demonstrated in the reference to Jesus as "Immanuel--God with us," and that is the concept of the immanence. One key thing He knows because of His divine nature, that we do not and cannot fully know because of our limited humanity, is the complete knowledge of the vast power of God to meet every need we could ever have. But, because He has come near through the Incarnation, He also knows the struggles of being human.

In a time of caregiving, it is especially meaningful to know that One Who knows exactly what it is like to be human has paved our way into the very presence of God. Jesus offers us strength because He knows what it is like to be weak. Our struggles are not something He takes lightly, because He knows what it is like to struggle. Because He is a High Priest Who has experienced hardship and suffering, He is able to compassionately speak on your behalf in the very presence of God the Father to make sure you have everything you need to accomplish your God-given tasks. He is praying for you even as you read this page. Take comfort in the fact that He is in the throne room right now, and He is on your side. Relish this Savior Who stands with you today. Close your book, close your eyes, and open yourself to receiving the answers to Jesus' prayers for you.

Day 4 Mark 6:30-32

I recently told a woman that I was leaving town for a short trip, as she was one of the people who would be on call in case my dad needed anything. There was some distracting noise, and so she missed part of what I said and asked, "Did you say you were going to be gone for a few months?" I paused. Another person pitched in and said, "No, he said he's leaving *in* a few *minutes*." But the response left me daydreaming about what it might be like to have a few months to just relax and rejuvenate. Real life, of course, was that it was just an overnight trip for business.   But didn't that idea sound wonderful to you, too? Wouldn't *you* like a month or two to just get away and rest?

One of the hardest aspects of caregiving is how tightly you are tied down. Respite care helps, assisting nurses help, and friends can help, but it still comes down to *you*. The responsibility remains yours.

Jesus knew the disciples could meet everybody's round the clock demands only for so long; then something had to give. And if something wasn't done to give the disciples some kind of break, it would be the disciples who would break instead. He insisted they get away from it all for a while to rest, renew and refresh.

You may not be able to literally get away since you probably have all sorts of pressures stressing you to the limit. A few minutes here and there can make all the difference in the world, whether reading these little devotions, or watching some clouds, or taking that afternoon nap. In all the scheduling that you do and that is thrust upon you, schedule some time for your own mental and spiritual health. It is essential not only for your own sanity, but also to enable you to be able to *effectively* continue your ministry of caregiving.

Day 5 Nehemiah 8:10

The work of a caregiver requires much strength. Not always so much physical strength, although even that depends on your specific situation. Lifting wheelchairs in and out of vehicles, or assisting a full size adult as they move from one place to another as they try to get out of bed or chairs can be physically taxing. However, more than physical strength, being a quality caregiver requires significant emotional and character strength.

Your emotional strength is what keeps everything from getting you down and driving you to discouragement or despair. Your character strength is what keeps you focused on the task at hand, when it seems no one understands or appreciates what you are doing. Character strength makes you the kind of person that someone is able to depend upon and trust.

In the daily drudgery of serving, it is easy to lose one's joy. But Nehemiah reminds us by his words and his example that in both the great and the tedious works of our lives, God's joy is the source of the strength we need. God's joy lifts our hearts and lightens our load. God's joy turns our work into two sided blessings: for us and for our charges. God's joy can outweigh the irritations and disappointments that come each day.

So how is your strength today? If strength has waned, could it be that you have lost touch with the joy that God promises to plant in our hearts? If so, then perhaps today could be a good day to create a joy list, reminding yourself of all the things about which you can rejoice, all the things God has done for you. It will keep you strong!

Day 6 John 5:2-9

If you to go Jerusalem today, you can see an excavated pit which is believed to be the place today's event occurred: the pool of Bethesda. Jesus approached this paralyzed man and asked if he wanted to be healed. The man's response was a description of how hard it was for him to lie there day after day, waiting for a chance to be healed and unable to get to the pool by himself. How discouraging that must have been for him. How frustrating to see others walk away healed, while he was regularly late in reaching the healing waters. It had to be especially frustrating to see others with friends or family nearby to help them at the perfect moment, while he lay there all alone.

You are in the role of helping a person such as this, someone unable to do for him/herself all of the things necessary to make life better. It is certainly a tough thing to care for people who have these debilitating illnesses or infirmities. But have you ever considered how hard it must also be for the person you assist, to not be able to do things that have always been simple for them, or that they know are so simple for many other people? It was frustrating for the man at the pool; it could well be as frustrating for the person in your charge.

There was great grace in the manner in which Jesus gently ministered to this frustrated and, in many ways, broken man as He restored him to wholeness. As you think of the awkwardness your charge may be experiencing, consider whether there might be ways to ease their frustration and discomfort at being so dependent on assistance for the daily tasks of life. It may be as simple as choosing not to do the tasks they could do for themselves, or having them assist with preparations for family dinners or household projects. Jesus did that for this struggling man, and as you do the same, you become a partner with Christ in a common ministry of making the lives of others just a little more bearable.

Day 7 Matthew 17:14-18

Caregiving for a loved one is something that comes as a shift in life, often unexpected, that has a stunning impact on the caregiver. A friend of mine was telling me about her experience when she served unexpectedly as the caregiver for her mother. It began the day her stepfather passed away, and, as she expressed it, "My life died. It changed the whole direction of my life." Some of it had to do with a lot of related circumstances, but suddenly she was thrust into the role of caregiver when she and her mother had expected something completely different. She instantly knew, though, that something had to be done. While another person might have walked away, she knew that the right thing for her was to step up to the task, even though it meant putting her career on hold, maybe never to be restarted. That is a tough shift to make, and emotionally, a very difficult one to handle.

The father in our passage today had his life altered by the fact that the expected child they celebrated was born with an illness that required constant attention. He turned to Jesus for help. Jesus met the need by healing the boy. Many caregivers, though, care for loved ones who do not experience this kind of healing, and find themselves providing care for a lifetime. In the meantime, we do what is necessary for the situation of our lives today. Not because we *have* to, but because we *choose* to. We choose to make caring for one we love a valued priority, knowing that Jesus *does* understand, and that the choice we have made is a noble one, even if unnoticed by the world.

MY PRAYER FOR YOU THIS WEEK

My prayer for you this week is that you will carry with you a deep sense of your partnership with God. May you sense his hands guiding yours as you reach out to minister to the one in your care. May your words truly impart the grace of God to all with whom you come in contact. May you glimpse a vision of God's love as you share that love in the ministry of caregiving. Amen.

Day 8   John 3:7-8

If you learn anything as a caregiver, you learn flexibility! In fact, whenever anyone asks me about plans for the week, my response is always that I don't plan much, because it can all change in a moment on any given day. In other words, I plan in tentative ways. Interestingly enough, the same thing is true when I plan my week while pastoring a church.

I like the conversation Jesus had with Nicodemus from which these verses are taken. The chapter contains some often quoted verses, including the beloved John 3:16. But today, I'd like to focus on the description of those born of the Spirit, and the movement of the Spirit of God. The words "invisible" and "unpredictable" come to mind. Free-flowing, swirling and shifting, adapting and moving...the Spirit of God works in God's own free-form fashion.

It seems to me that we can learn a lot about how the Spirit works by observing how God makes adjustments in our daily schedules as we do the work of caregiving. Many a time I had plans for the day, only to find myself at the emergency room or running a dozen errands instead. I had to adjust. I had to be flexible. I had to allow my life to be shaped by forces outside of myself. And I had to do it in a way that did not communicate disappointment, displeasure or frustration, lest those I cared for feel guilty or burdensome. The truth is, those adjusting circumstances themselves were very likely the Spirit's way of guiding me onto the appropriate path for the day. If I had been rigid in my schedule and refused to adapt, I would have missed the opportunities to serve as I did, opportunities to let my parents know they were loved.

And so, if you are going to live a life under the guidance of the Holy Spirit, probably the best characteristic you can acquire is the ability to be flexible!

Day 9 John 14:25-27

Peace. Does that sound like a foreign word to you these days? I was down at a friend's lake cabin recently, seeking a weekend away for some basic peace and quiet. There was a brief snowfall that coated the trees and ground very beautifully. It was so quiet and peaceful to just stop and look out over the serene setting. These days getaway opportunities like that are rare. And the peace such a getaway provides is transitory...refreshing, but short lived.

In contrast, the peace Jesus promises doesn't require a getaway, nor is it so illusory. The peace Jesus gives is available for us *in the midst* of life's hubbub. It is a peace that remains deep within as something that centers us, filling us with a sense of assurance and purpose in life, even though we may be frantically dealing with tasks that demand our attention. It is a peace that reminds us we are loved; a peace that comes from knowing that no matter what happens, our eternal destiny is secure, a peace that comes from knowing one is doing the very tasks God has called us to do. We have Jesus' peace, knowing we do not handle our struggles alone, but that God has promised that He will be with us to see us through.

What do you need to do today, to get in touch with the peace Christ promises for you? Instead of spending a lot of time reading this book, do *that!*

Day 10 Psalm 121

You can feel very alone when you are a primary caregiver and on call 24/7...which, in fact, in many ways you are. As you care for the person in your charge, you may find yourself watching all the time...and asking yourself questions. "Are they getting too near the hot stove? Have they gotten into something that could be dangerous for them? Do they need help getting up or coming back from the other room? Is there anything on the floor in front of them that could trip them? Are their steps steady, or do I need to be ready to catch them?" Lots of questions for the cautious caregiver.

In today's passage the message is unequivocally clear: you are not the only one who watches. Not only that, but even when you are not able to watch every single minute and every single movement (and realistically, you simply cannot), remember this: God *never* sleeps. He is the One Who watches each of us every single moment of every day. He watches over you as you look out for your charge, and He watches over the charge when you cannot. In some ways in fact, as you watch over someone you love, you are very much acting like God. Just realize though, you aren't God; you can't be everywhere and do everything all the time. Rest in the fact that God is with you in the process of watching over the ones you love, and that He watches over them as well, for He loves you both.

Day 11 Hebrews 10:35-37

Endurance. Boy, if there is anything a caregiver needs, it is endurance. Day after day, week after week, month after month, the details and responsibilities pile up and just keep on piling! Some days you can feel as though all you are doing is trudging along!

I've never run a marathon, but that sure sounds like a good parallel to me. They have to push on through the wall, they say, to make it to the end. I have had times when I have pushed myself to finish climbing a mountain, or hiking a trail. I also do a lot of home improvement projects, some of which seem to have innumerable details that arise as the work progresses. Sometimes it gets so frustrating that it becomes difficult to keep at the project until it is done. But the satisfaction comes when the job is done and I can stand back to admire the completed project and the difference it makes.

This passage in Hebrews is talking about enduring and persevering in doing the will of God until we receive the ultimate reward. The lesson applies to our lives in caregiving specifically, as well, because if caring for a dear person in need isn't part of God's will, then I don't know what is! God promises rewards, and I believe that one of life's greatest rewards is the great satisfaction that comes from knowing you have made somebody's life a little more tolerable, a bit safer, and helped them know they are loved as you cared for them in their time of need. It requires endurance, but it is well worth the race.

Day 12 Philippians 2:3-4

These verses seem so backwards, don't they? At least it may seem that way from the perspective of your current situation. That is, in this passage Paul challenges us to pay attention to the needs of other people, not just to our own needs. But really, isn't that what you spend most of your time doing these days? Don't you sometimes feel that you need a verse that encourages you to not just look out for the needs of others, but also to your own needs? I know I have.

God *does* understand that we each have needs. In fact, in passages like Matthew 6:25-33, He makes clear that He is personally concerned about even our most basic needs. But far too many of us get caught up in the temptation to be so wrapped up in our own needs and our own little circle that we forget to be concerned about the needs of others. Yet Jesus' command that we love others as ourselves demands that we be concerned about the lives of others.

One of the great things about being a caregiver is that you are learning by practice what it truly means to be looking out for the needs of others. Not only that, but when you feel as though you aren't accomplishing much, you can take note of the fact that you are daily fulfilling the command of today's scripture. Knowing that you are being obedient in this, you can also know that God is pleased.

Day 13 Hebrews 13:15

Is life tough for you these days? Are there times when you feel weary, beaten, or maybe just long for a break? Maybe you are feeling overwhelmed and stressed with so many things waiting for your attention. Maybe you have days you feel trapped in your situation, or robbed of opportunities in life. Maybe you even feel financially stressed, as you find your funds are stretched to the extreme...or beyond! Any of these can occur in the process of caregiving. If you haven't felt that way yet, realize there may be days like that ahead; it just comes with the territory.

If any of those apply to you, then today's passage is for you! Can you praise God for the situation you are in? For the fact that God knows where you are, and intends good things for you in the midst of it? For the fact that God has compassion, strength and purpose for you in this time? Can you offer praise that a perfect plan is being worked out for your life, and that the plan leads to the throne room of heaven through Jesus? And praise for how much He loves you, with all your failings and foibles?

Especially in those times when it is hard to give praise, your praise becomes one of the most precious sacrifices

God ever receives. Today might be a good day to make such a sacrifice. What do you think?

Day 14 2 Kings 5:1-7

I kind of feel sorry for this king, don't you? There he was sitting on his throne, doing royal things all day long, being treated as a son of privilege, when this very sick guy showed up bringing gold and silver. When Jehoram, the king, heard that the man indicated he was seeking healing for his disease and had brought the treasure as payment, the king suddenly panicked. Was it a ploy to start a war? What in the world gave this guy the idea that the king could heal him? Trapped in a corner, there was no good answer; after all, he was a KING, not a miracle worker!

Then the rescue came.   He received a message from Elisha requesting that the man be sent over to him, with full conviction that God was able to accomplish the miracle sought. The story ends happily as the man received his healing when he followed the prophet's advice.

Have you ever felt like King Jehoram, as you serve as caregiver? Like you are being asked to perform miracles, and know that you are already stretched to your limits, that some things are simply beyond your ability. It may be that you are asked to give advice in areas you do not feel competent. It may be that the emotional toll it takes leaves you stressed and exhausted. In fact, you might actually feel like crying out at times, "I am doing the best I can. I can't work miracles, you know." Then perhaps, like King Jehoram should have, you might want to reflect on the fact that you really are not expected by God to act beyond your ability, anyway. God asks you to allow Him to use you as you do your best, and then trust that He can use other individuals and other means to fill up the needs you cannot. It never hurts to remind yourself that God doesn't expect you to do everything...just to do your part.

MY PRAYER FOR YOU THIS WEEK

My prayer for you this week is for God's strength to fill you whenever you experience your own strength waning. May you find the opportunity for rest to bring renewal. May God show you new ways to tap into his strength as you seek him, day by day. Amen.

Day 15 1 Samuel 24:1-11

Saul was a man who somehow had gotten himself obsessed with a vendetta against David. He feared David's righteousness, and that David would one day become king instead of his own son, Jonathan. On one of his mad hunts after David, David ends up hiding in a cave at the same time that Saul happens to decide to use that very cave as an outhouse. David was trapped, in peril, but also had an opportunity to end the battle or to set a godly and noble example. That is what he chose: he spared Saul's life when he could easily have killed him, while also retaining evidence of his action to show it to Saul.

You may feel trapped in all the activities of caregiving, much as David was trapped in that cave, with no good options for escape. And in it, there may be people attacking you as well, complaining about your decisions and the way you do things. It can feel as if you are being cornered with no good way out. As you respond to those around you...even your critics...seek to be like David by showing mercy to others and not attempting to get even by taking some sort of revenge.

If you feel as if you have been trapped in stifling responsibilities, realize that it is only for a season. Many of us are in our situation because of choices we made, even though we may not have realized all of the implications when we chose. Deliverance will come at the right time and way by the hand of God, rather than through something we concoct ourselves. So if you feel that you are shut into a dark cave for now, it is okay. You are not alone there, and God will not leave you in it forever.

Day 16 Proverbs 27:1

I took my 94 year old dad to see a movie yesterday. He is the one I am responsible to care for at this time. The movie was about World War II, in which he served, and he had expressed an interest in seeing it. I was a little concerned, as he had already had a pretty full day, and I hesitated to risk wearing him out. On the other hand, he was feeling good yesterday, and his health has been up and down enough that I wasn't sure he would be as strong if I waited for another day. So we went.

A lot of your life as a caregiver may be like that these days. You have today. You have the condition you and your charge are in today. You don't know for sure what tomorrow will be like, so don't assume. When you are a caregiver, especially if your charge's health is precarious, you have to deal with each day as it comes. Opportunities to rejuvenate yourself, as well as opportunities to enjoy time with the one you love contain no guarantees for the future. (Actually, that is true with all those we love...we just don't acknowledge it unless we come face to face with that reality.) Always remember: you do not know tomorrow, so deal wisely with today. Don't put off anything until a tomorrow that may not come.

Day 17 Exodus 20:8-11

Do you suppose God was tired after six days of creating? After all, based on what science teaches us about how complicated the microcosm is and how vast the expansive universe is, creating it all was certainly a pretty huge project! But then, God is pretty powerful.

No, God wasn't particularly tired; nothing in the Bible indicates that He was. In fact, Psalm 121 specifically indicates that God *doesn't* slumber or sleep. *And yet*, God's example teaches and commands *us* that it is *critical* for the cycle of life to regularly include a space and time for rest. And I would suggest that is especially true for you as a caregiver.

Huge demands are made on your time, energy and resources every single day, sometimes 24/7. There are those who suggest that there are more like 36 hours' worth of demands, or that most 24 hour periods can feel like weeks! These things seem to push us beyond what God commanded us to do when He established a Sabbath rest every seventh day. I am not speaking in some legalistic way of tracking time, so much as I am about the importance of the value of regular rest, renewal and worship in our lives.

If your life has spun out of control and your schedule overloaded, I want to encourage you today to start developing a plan to make a way, *a regularly scheduled way*, to create rest in the daily and weekly cycle of your life. Let caregiving be your vocation, calling or act of service at this time, but do NOT let it rob you of all life by denying you a space for rest. Even if your only rest might be five minutes behind a closed bedroom door. Make resting your mind, your body and your spirit a personal priority, so that you will be a better caregiver.

Day 18 Psalm 91:1-6

Do you have memories of snuggling up in your mother's or father's lap as a child, perhaps crying because you were afraid or hurt? Maybe you have done the same as an adult with someone who has loved you: gone to that person and shared your struggle, feeling their arms wrapped around you to give comfort and encouragement as you wept. In such times, that is one of the most powerful and reassuring experiences you can have. It just feels good to have somebody's arms around you, as if that person could protect you from "the big bad wolves" that are waiting to devour you.

That, for me, is the image of today's passage, with God as my refuge. Under His wings, safe and secure from any harm that might come my way. Or in His shadow, where the scorching heat of summer cannot burn. The sense that God is surrounding me, protecting me, comforting me and offering Himself as a refuge from all the terrible pestilences this world can bring is something that makes a tremendous difference when I feel I cannot handle life's challenges alone. Because I know I do not *have* to handle them alone. And because I know that anything that touches me must first pass though the protective shield of God's love and plan.

On a cold wintry night, there is nothing more soothing than sitting in front of a blazing fire, snuggled up under a blanket with someone who loves you. *Except* snuggling up under the wings of the Almighty.

Day 19 Galatians 5:22-23

I don't know about you, but when I read over this list of all these incredible attributes God's Spirit seeks to manifest in our lives, I am reminded of how far I am from the perfect love of God. Not that I can manufacture any of this manifestation of Christlikeness myself, but somehow I have to learn how to let the Spirit use me and be open to the changes He wants to make in my life. I have found that the activity of caregiving is the perfect place to experience the arranging of the fruit-basket of my heart. For example, in caregiving, I have lots of opportunities to be gentle or patient. Then again, I'd say kindness is the hallmark of great caregiving, wouldn't you agree? Or maybe faithfulness, as you continue to stand by this person day after day, or year after year.

Well, you can read and consider the list yourself. But the sum of it all is that caregiving is like a long term apprenticeship in the school of love, as manifested in the class on patience, the experiment in faithfulness and the time spent training on the job in the field of kindness. As you are going through this time of education and growth, I encourage you to do your best to see to it that when this caregiving time is over, you will graduate with highest honors!

Day 20 Luke 1:30-32 and Matthew 1:20-21

Okay, so I don't know about you, but I think it would have been pretty intimidating to be Mary or Joseph! What would it have felt like to hear God saying through His angels, "Okay you guys, I'm going to send My divine son as your baby, and I want you two to be responsible to take care of Him and to raise Him and teach Him everything He needs to know to manage down there"? Gulp. Can you imagine?

God knows the weakness and fallibility of humanity. With that in mind, there must have been something pretty special about Mary and Joseph for Him to know that, with His help, their new family was the right place for Jesus to be born. He must have seen something in the kind of people they were that convinced Him He could count on them to do a good job with Jesus. I mean, you just can't go putting the Son of God, Savior of the World, Prince of Peace into any old home and think He is going to be properly cared for, now can you? Nope, God must have thought a great deal of Mary and Joseph. And maybe the main thing He saw was that they were the kind of people who knew they would need and seek God's help. Even the angel said that Mary was highly favored and Elizabeth called described her as most blessed among women. Something pretty special, indeed.

I think God also has the same attitude about you, something special that convinces Him you are the kind of person who can capably care for the well-being of another one of his creations. Not everybody could do what you are doing. I have known people who have openly admitted it. And I have known individuals being cared for who have commented themselves that certain family members could care for their special needs while others would not be able to do so. Nope, it isn't a mistake God has placed this person in your care. God sees something in *you*; otherwise He wouldn't have allowed you to be doing what you are doing. It is quite a ministry, isn't it? And quite an honor. Do your best to not let Him down, realizing that He knows you just as you are. He doesn't expect perfection...only that you do your best.

Day 21 2 Corinthians 12:7-10

Paul had problems in life. Lots of them. Disasters struck in the form of things like shipwrecks, people who attacked and harassed him, friends who turned against him...his life was no cushy experience with God protecting him from any kind of hardship.

There was something he desperately wanted God to lift from him. Some believed it was an illness or physical infirmity. I know some who aren't so sure of that who think the thorn in his flesh was that there were individuals who followed him and opposed his work everywhere he went. It doesn't matter. (Actually, I believe if it was important for us to know, God would have made sure the specifics were included!) What *does* matter is what Paul learned in the midst of it: that God's grace is sufficient for whatever it was Paul faced. Some interpret this passage to mean that through the grace of God Paul would be able to make it through whatever he faced. Some suggest that God is reminding Paul that God's grace is already made available, and that taking hold of God's power by faith would not only get Paul through it, but enable him to conquer the situation! Regardless, God's grace is the means by which God gives us exactly what we need to face whatever life may bring.

There is enough of God's grace for you, as well. God may have been implying that if Paul would tap into God's grace, he would conquer whatever the issue was and drive it away. *Or* God may have been saying that Paul didn't need to worry about getting away from the struggle, because God's grace would help him face it and accept it as his plight in life. Again, it doesn't matter which way it ended up for Paul; what matters is the sufficiency of God's grace, because whichever way his life would go, God's grace would keep him going. Paul's understanding of his hardship was transformed from something that was an awful plague into an opportunity for his own weakness to show so that God's power might be revealed.

MY PRAYER FOR YOU THIS WEEK

My prayer for you this week is that you will be able to catch just a glimpse of the priceless value of the work that you do. As you do the hundreds of little things that nobody notices, may you sense God's eyes watching every effort, and building those tasks into heavenly treasure. Amen.

Day 22 John 10:27-29

Are you sure of your place in the Father's hand? What about the one you care for, is that person sure, too? Have you had a conversation together about this issue? Sometimes, knowledge of one's eternal destiny can be the "elephant in the room," as individuals who both know that one of them is facing death, carefully avoid raising a topic that might sound too morbid or create the impression of having given up. Nevertheless, it is an important conversation to have. In fact, it can actually be a relief to have cleared the air on the topic of eternal destiny with someone you care about and who cares about you.

That conversation can have great impact on a looming funeral service, as well as your own sense of peace after your loved one is gone. It can also make a big difference in your own sense of assurance as you move on in life. Most importantly, it may be the conversation that prepares the way to heaven for someone who may not have been sure before.

At the same time, the fact that you are reading this devotional demonstrates that you know that the spiritual life is about more than eternal destiny; it is also about a growing relationship with God day by day as we face whatever life brings. There may be other topics that you may want to discuss as well. Several times over the years my father and I have discussed such things as God's purpose at this time of his life, the spiritual condition of those he loves, the future of his church and questions he had about various passages of scripture he was reading...we even discussed what kinds of things he might do to help make a difference for others now. As a result, he adopted a ministry of sending anniversary, birthday, sympathy and get well cards to others in the congregation. There may be issues related to God's forgiveness the individual is struggling with as he or she contemplates eternity. There may be requests for time with a pastor. There may be a desire for prayer together. If you are willing to open the discussion, you might be surprised at the opportunities that arise.

In the time of struggle that requires the receiving and giving of care, it can be a great thing to be reminded that, even in this extremity, you both are safe in the hands of God. It can be a precious time of spiritual connections and growth. Today's passage so clearly reminds us that God can keep us safe in His hand forever, no matter what this life brings.

Day 23 2 Timothy 4:9-12

Have you ever noticed all the names of people who traveled with Paul? Sometimes he mentions them at the beginning of his letters, including them as people who are sending the notes. In other letters, he ends by mentioning the people by name and including their greetings to the recipients. In his second letter to Timothy, he specifically mentioned that almost everybody had left him, and that he longed for company.

Today, we would call those people his "ministry team," or his "support group." Paul handled some pretty tough experiences in life, far tougher than anything I have had to endure. With all the hard things he faced, Paul was smart enough not to try to do it alone. He gathered his prayer partners, his co-workers, his traveling companions and his advisors to help him be able to do the work he was called to do.

Are you trying to do everything alone? Oh, I know that many of the tasks of a caregiver *are* things that you just have to do by yourself. *However*, doing those by yourself is different from doing them alone. There is a reason support groups exist, and I strongly encourage you to find one. Maybe you are part of an organized support group, like those for families of Alzheimer's patients. Maybe your support group is much more informal. Maybe there are family members with whom you discuss major decisions before making them. Maybe there are friends at church or in your small group and you are able to confide prayer concerns in that context. Maybe you could unload occasionally with a friend over a cup of coffee.

Whatever support network works for you, make sure you keep it in place, so that it will be there when you really need it during times of hardship and struggle. If you don't have such a network, then it might help to realize that you don't *have* to go it alone. There are people who care about you. Share your world with them, ask for some of their time. Don't lose touch with them. If you are feeling a big ragged today, then this would be a good day to make one of those contacts and catch up a bit.

Day 24 John 13:5-17

This is one of the most beloved images from the story of the Last Supper. The disciples couldn't believe Jesus was doing what He was doing when He washed their feet. He was their leader, their teacher, their Messiah, the One Who gave them hope and meaning. And here He was, washing their feet, the kind of job left for the lowest servants to do. It was a dirty, smelly job.

Some churches have services in which they also wash feet, sometimes at Easter. I was at a church once where the church leaders and spouses did so for a Maundy Thursday service. But it isn't the same as what Jesus did, because everybody at the service had been wearing socks or hose and shoes, not bare feet in sandals on dusty roads traveled by man and beast alike. It wasn't a pleasant job in Jesus' day.

In modern terms, what Jesus did is more like the kind of tasks nurses' aides perform in hospitals and nursing homes. Even the nurses would prefer somebody else did the tasks! It is also like what you are doing. The passage ends with Jesus saying that we are to be serving in the same manner

He did that night. That means you are in pretty good company as you humbly and faithfully do the daily drudgery tasks that are part of caregiving. Good for you! Good work!

Day 25 Romans 8:26-27

Have you ever heard a *perfect* prayer? What does that idea even mean to you? "A perfect prayer." Kind of an interesting notion, huh? I would like to make what might be a stunning suggestion: God hears perfect prayers all the time! No, He really does! Because every prayer offered by one of His people, is supplemented by the Holy Spirit's work on our behalf to polish and perfect it on the way to the ear of God. And so, based on scriptures like this one, I believe that by the time God hears our cries, the Spirit truly has polished them into perfection. (I also believe He does the same thing with the songs of praise we sing...which is really good news for someone with a voice like mine!)

This can be a very encouraging notion, because if you are like me at all, it is frequently difficult to even know what our prayers should be when we are serving as a caregiver. "God, heal this person I care for?" "God, take them home, so they suffer no more?" "God, send somebody else to take over, so that I can have a break?" "God, show me whether I need to look into using a care facility or continue to care for this person at home?" "God, do I need to consider another physician?" You know the prayers. But there may be other things to consider with regard to our prayers.

It is okay if you have a hard time finding the words, and aren't exactly sure what you should even be asking. Maybe the exact wording isn't so important after all. As a believer, God's Spirit is involved with every prayer you offer, and can guide your prayers and shape them as they approach the throne of God. So maybe it is more important that you take time to listen for the Spirit's guidance as you frame your prayers. Then, even if you don't have clarity as you pray, you can trust His work to make every single one of your prayers "perfect."

Day 26 Genesis 9:12-16

As I write this day's entry, it is springtime where I live. Spring means rain, often in the form of thunderstorms. And it means beautiful rainbows. In the story of Noah, the rainbow is presented as a token of promise, the promise that God will never again destroy humanity by flooding the earth. I don't know if that is why I love rainbows or not, but I do love the beauty they bring to a stormy sky. There have been many times I have seen radiant rainbows, even double rainbows, and grabbed my camera to try to preserve the image.

I don't know what your experience with promises has been, but I know some people have kept their promises to me, and some have not. I have learned with some people to take their promises with a grain of salt. On the other hand, I am sure there have been things I have said that have been taken as promises, maybe even made as promises, which I haven't always followed through on, in spite of the best of intentions. That's probably true of you, as well, I bet. But God is different. When *God* promises something...well, that's something you can count on. His reputation is on the line, and He is pretty careful about His reputation for faithfulness to fulfill His promises.

It is a pretty amazing thing that God chooses to make promises to us in the first place. After all, He is certainly under no obligation to do so. He chooses to do so because it is His nature to be loving and giving. He also chooses to do so because we are not so good at trusting, and sometimes that promise is just enough to cause us to take the chance and take Him up on His offer. And I am especially touched when I see rainbows, because they always remind me of a God Who makes promises for us.

Perhaps somewhere today you might see a rainbow in the sky, or images of rainbows in photographs. If so, let it be a symbol that God has made promises to *you* as well. If you don't see one today, then perhaps the next time you see one, you will use it as an opportunity to remember His promises. Regardless, I invite you to take a moment to recall some of God's promises that have had special meaning for *your* life. If you have time, look up and read the passages telling of the rainbow once again, just as a reminder. (If you can't remember any, some special promises are provided in Appendix 1.)

Let the assurance of those meaningful promises nourish your spirit today. Maybe you could make some sort of reminders for yourself that you will notice in your daily routine. You might even draw a little rainbow on them. God always remembers His promises to us. Sometimes, though, *we* need to be reminded that they are there for us to claim.

Day 27 Acts 20:34-35

Every once in a while when I am with friends, the subject gets around to such things as helping at nursing homes or senior citizen centers, or doing jail ministries or maybe volunteering at a camp for kids...something like that. And then some individual who regularly does one of these things will comment that whenever they go, they come away feeling that they got more than they gave. They will also say that their intention was to bless the other people, but that they were more blessed themselves. Have you ever heard somebody say that, too?

Okay, I will admit that sometimes I am skeptical of such comments. Sometimes I wonder if it is a genuine statement, or whether the person is just trying to sound pious or something. And yet, I know it really does happen that way sometimes...I have even experienced it myself.

Right now, you are potentially in such a situation. You may feel as though you give and you give and you give... sometimes to the point that you think there is no more *left* to give. But have you ever considered that with every gift of yourself that you give, you are reaping blessings untold? Some of them are blessings you know and experience here in this life as you do the tasks; others you will only realize several years down the road; and some are not going to be seen until viewed in glory.

I have had the privilege of caring for my mother and father in their final years. Just yesterday, my wife and I were driving through a nearby city, and I told her of a special memory I had of a restaurant there, because of a memory of being there with my mother near the end of her life. Hard though some of the caregiving time has been, I would not trade those special memories and opportunities for anything, would you? It truly *is* a blessing to be doing what you are doing, and sometimes, it helps to just remember that.

Day 28 John 19:1-11

At the trial, Pilate informed Jesus that he had the authority to release or to crucify him. In other words, the decision regarding Jesus' life or death was in Pilate's hands. Jesus, in turn, responded that Pilate would have no such authority had it not been given to him by God. Probably not the way *Pilate* thought he had gotten the job of making life and death decisions.

I have been the one to take my father to the hospital emergency room a number of times in recent years while other family members were living at a distance.

Frequently, I have suddenly found myself in a situation where I was asked for a decision by doctors and other hospital personnel. Most of the choices have been simple ones to make, especially when the individual was merely seeking information or general guidance. But every once in a while, the decision has had greater significance. Sometimes it has felt as though the choice I had to make carried the kind of medical risk that could have been a death sentence, while other times I felt that the choice provided a gift of extended or better life. Either way, it has not always been an easy task. Perhaps you know all too well the experiences I am talking about.

As caregiver you bear a great deal of responsibility, and part of that responsibility is to make choices that may not always be easy. Sometimes you have time to consult with family members and experts to help guide you in your decisions. Other times there is not enough time for much consultation and you are called upon to choose in an instant...even choices that may literally be life and death decisions for the one in your care.

I encourage you to always keep a breath of prayer around each decision. I encourage you to consult and include others in the process whenever you can. I encourage you to be brave as you make the tough decisions, not overreaching in a mad rush, but also not shying away from the hard questions. And I encourage you to be brave enough to discuss the key issues with your loved one and your family well in advance of having to make such decisions. In my own experience, I found that having those conversations in advance gave me a great deal of confidence in the decisions I was making, even if I knew the decision might end up being the last one I make for my loved one. One day it may well be the last such decision you make, as it once was for me as well. If you seek him, you can trust that God will help you through each and every decision you make.

MY PRAYER FOR YOU THIS WEEK

My prayer for you this week is that somewhere in the hustle and bustle of the daily activities you do, you will encounter surprise moments of unspeakable peace, fully aware that they are sacred moments and that you are nestled in God's loving arms. Amen.

Day 29 1 Peter 5:7

Well, how is life these days? Any cares or anxieties? And how are you doing at obeying this verse? *Especially* when you focus on the word "all"? There are just *so* many cares when you are a caregiver. Do you feel that you are ever able to really cast *all* of them onto God?

Cares and anxieties are a regular part of life here on earth. They come our way on a daily, even an hourly basis. They accompany responsibilities that are ours as well as the uncertainties of the unknown futures that may be outside of our control. In life, the question isn't whether or not we have cares and anxieties that come to us. It is a question of what we do with them once they come. We can choose to let our minds dwell on them perpetually. We can choose to turn a blind eye, and pretend like we don't care. We can let them consume us, paralyze us with fear and disturb our sleep. Or we can learn what Peter meant when he invites us to cast them on God. So which best describes you? Have you developed the habit of casting those burdensome cares onto the God Who cares for you?

Maybe today you could at least start the process. What cares and anxieties weigh heaviest on your heart today? How about taking a minute to tell God two specifically right now? After all, the truth is that God loves you a great deal, and He wants to be *your* caregiver, even as you are imitating Him in your giving of care to the one *you* love.

With every smile, every touch, every deed you do, every word of encouragement you offer in your caregiving, remember that God is *caring* for *you*, too. And also remember, God's care is there even if, perhaps like your loved one, you don't really understand why He does everything He is doing for you just now. Trust that He is a *good* caregiver. In fact, *He's the best caregiver of all!*

Day 30 Exodus 33:13-15

For Moses, it was critical to have a deep contact with God if He was going to try to lead these people through the wilderness. In response to that need, God promised that His very presence would go with Moses and the people every step of the way through the wilderness. In his reply, Moses made plain that if God wasn't going to go with them through it all, then he didn't even want to go.

God has promised to walk with you and me, as well. His presence can be found every time you open your Bible, enter into worship, celebrate the Lord's Supper or bow down in prayer. But the truth is His presence is there even when we are changing the sheets or doing the laundry or pushing the wheelchair. It was critical for Moses that he really know that God was with him every step of the way. How critical is it for you? Are you letting God know how important it is that He help you manage all that you have to manage, each and every day, as you wander through the challenges facing you? I think God was pleased Moses wanted Him to go along. And I think He would be pleased to know that you do, as well.

Today might be a good day to discuss with God the areas of your life that are impacted by His presence, and the ones in which you desire to have a better awareness that

He is there. You could also invite Him into specific areas of your life, or specific tasks you face each day. Maybe what is needed is not so much prayer seeking His presence as reminders that He is with you. Are there some ways you could build some reminders into your day today that will help you realize that God is present? Perhaps writing out on a card the verse from today that promises God's presence and then posting it on a mirror, placing it in your pocket or somewhere else you will encounter it throughout the day. Maybe the best way to remember God's presence is to bear witness to others about God's work in your life. Or you may be one of those people who find journaling a helpful exercise. In caregiving, you may not always have time at the end or start of the day to write much in a journal. If not, then carrying a little notepad or starting a file on your computer might provide a place where you could jot down some quick notes when God does something special for you that reveals His presence. Could you make time today to call a friend and discuss with them the difference God is making for you? As you do so, you might want to also share some prayer requests for ways you need God's help more.

With every smile, every touch, every deed you do, every word of encouragement you offer in your caregiving, remember that God is caring for *you*, too. And remember, God's care is there even if, perhaps like your loved one, you don't really understand why He does everything He is doing for you just now. Trust that He is a *good* caregiver. In fact, *He's the best caregiver of all!*

Day 31   1 Corinthians 10:31 and Ephesians 6:5-8

There are people who are totally oblivious to what your life is like as a caregiver. There are others, perhaps, who have some knowledge of what you are doing, and are very impressed. If you try to do everything you are doing so that everybody will be pleased with what you are doing, you will have taken on an impossible task. You will also have missed the point of what you are doing, and the point of life itself.

The Ephesians passage is a section addressed to those who served as slaves in Roman society, but it also applies to us as slaves of Christ.   The Corinthian passage is taken from a discussion of the debates about Christians and dietary restrictions in a pagan and idolatrous society. These two topics provide the context for Paul to state a common and key biblical principle: our lives are to be lived in such a way that God is glorified by everything we say and do. That includes the way we perform our tasks as caregivers.

As you do the thankless tasks, and as you do the delightful things you enjoy doing with your loved one, remember who you are actually doing them for. Yes, you are doing these things for the sake of this person in need of care and support. But ultimately, you are doing them for God. Do them with an awareness that God is constantly watching you, and will reward you according to your deeds. Do your tasks with an awareness that people are also watching you, and in some cases are drawing conclusions about God and about Christianity based on what they see in you. Do your tasks as offerings to God, as if you were doing them for God Himself, or with a special commission from God.   These perspectives change everything about caregiving, because they change caregiving from merely a stressful job into an eternal service. You are called to glorify God in each and every thing you do as a caregiver or anything else that you do, every day of your life.

Day 32 1 Kings 19:1-8

Ever feel overwhelmed? Actually, a more profound question for caregivers is, "Do you ever *not* feel overwhelmed?" It can really wear on you after a while, can't it? It can make you withdraw into yourself, or feel as though you want to just run away because you can't take it anymore.

That is how Elijah felt. And he *did* run away. Having won a great victory after having stood strong against an evil king and queen for *years*, Elijah just was not ready to handle another round of attacks by his nemesis, Jezebel. He left. He headed back out to the wilderness, away from it all. Something that is not quite as easily done when there is someone depending on you day by day. (Whenever you have the opportunity to get away for a couple of days, though, it is a good thing to do!)

Today, I want to point out that there are a few things worth noticing with regard to this story. First, you aren't the only person to feel overwhelmed, or to long to just get away from it all for a bit, somehow. Second, God was willing to meet Elijah out where he was, to provide for him as he sought respite in the midst of his stress. And third, once Elijah got back a little strength, God sent him back to the roots of his faith, back to the mountain where Moses received the first covenant. If you are overwhelmed, realize God is willing to meet with you just as you are, and that taking the time to remember your roots may be just the ticket to get you back on your feet.

Day 33 Ephesians 6:1-3

Paul referred to this commandment as the first commandment with a promise. There is a promised reward for obedience to this command: life will go well with you. Not that it will be easy, but that what it is will be truly good.

I moved back to my hometown when the need and opportunity arose, as my parents were aging. This commandment brought itself to the forefront of my mind in a way it never had before. What is more honoring of your parents than giving of yourself in their time of need, to make sure they have what they need in their lives? Over these years, I have often thought of the fact that they did so much to care and provide for me when I was just a child, that returning the favor at this stage of their lives was the least I could do. It has been a decision that has been meaningful and rewarding, even though it brought with it significant difficulties and uncertainty.

You may be caring for parents, another relative, or the person you care for may be someone unrelated. If you are caring for parents at this time of your life, then I encourage you to view your task as fulfilling this commandment of God. Don't merely do the things you do because they need to be done or out of some sense of familial obligation. Instead, do them as an offering to God, and an exercise in obedience to God's command. And whenever you get discouraged, hang on to the promise attached to the command that Paul mentioned. For those of you whose caregiving is for someone other than a parent, then you might want to consider that God may well see what you are doing as going above and beyond the call of duty. We came to this role in a variety of ways, for a variety of relationships. Regardless of how we got here, caregiving is a ministry that is surely close to the heart of God. I believe that for all of us caregivers, the greatest reward we could ever have will be the smile on God's face.

Day 34 2 Samuel 18:19-23, 28-29

If you want your lawnmower fixed, or want something done on your car, you should not bring it to me. I don't do those things. Oh, sometimes I try. And there are a few things I can do. But I am not a mechanically-minded person, and the limits of my expertise are fairly close at hand. It simply isn't my gift; that is the role of other gifted people. So if you asked me to fix your lawnmower, I would most likely turn you down, and refer you to somebody who will work on it in such a way that it will run afterwards!

It is easy to identify these kinds of skills and limits. It is not so easy to identify them when it comes to caregiving. Especially when it comes to our limits. Far too many caregivers keep giving and giving, until they are left a physical and/or emotional wreck themselves, sometimes never recovering. They were unable to identify their limits or, having identified them, were unable to abide by them. I know several individuals who had a hard time admitting they could no longer do the caregiving task. It had become more than their skills, time, or physical and emotional strength would allow, and yet they felt that to place their loved one in a care facility was some kind of betrayal.

I would like to suggest an alternative to you. The young man in today's story wanted so badly to be the one to carry the news of the victory over David's rebellious son to David, but he was not really experienced enough to know how to handle such a responsibility well. After all, the squashing of the rebellion meant the death of David's son, and that is a delicate matter to report. At first he wasn't permitted to go, but finally Joab relented, the young man outran the experienced messenger but found himself at a loss of words when he stood in front of the king to give his account.

Well, just as the messenger in today's story got himself in over his head, and flubbed the whole task when it really mattered, it also does not help us to take on more than we can really do. The experienced messenger who arrived after him knew what he was doing, and with the right words, effectively accomplished the mission. In the United States where I live, there are caregiving people who know what they are doing...it is their specialty, their profession, and they have the appropriate staff to cover the task, rather than one person trying to do it all. I leave working on my lawnmowers to people who know more than I do, and I have learned there are times that I am not able to do some of the tasks of caregiving as well as those trained personnel can, either. I had to learn those limits by experience, because I sometimes overestimated my time or underestimated the task. Whichever way you learn it, it is an important thing to learn.

Once, while caregiving for my father, he developed some kind of illness, and though I intended on having him stay at my home, it quickly became apparent it required more ability than I had. So he went into a care facility for short term rehab. In a few days, his temperature took an upward turn, not a big one, but a definite turn. The nurse on duty caught it, called me, and urged me to take him to the emergency room (it was nighttime). That action saved his life. Literally. It turned out to be a serious condition. Had he still been at my home, I would not have even thought to take his temperature or, if I had, would not have thought anything about the mild fever beyond pulling out pain relievers from the medicine chest. It was beyond my expertise.

He was safer and better cared for at that facility than if I had, in my misguided concept of love, tried to take care of him myself. The truly loving thing was to make sure he had the care he needed. Sometimes I was able to provide that care, but other times it was beyond my ability and would require the help of others. I urge you to also consider that there may be times or situations in which it is actually more loving to NOT be the primary caregiver, even though it may not feel that way to you at the time. Ask God to give you the discernment you will need to make that distinction.

Day 35 1 Samuel 1:1-8

It was very hard for Hannah, not being able to have a child in a culture where having children was closely tied to the value of a woman. Especially when she had to put up with taunting from Elkanah's other wife, Peninnah, who had borne him several children. (Of course, if he had only taken one wife in the first place, there wouldn't have been this taunting....)

But it was also difficult for Elkanah. It was hard to see this woman he loved struggle, and suffer the abuse. I wonder if he ever scolded Peninnah for her behavior. In any case, he was clearly aware it was difficult for Hannah, and so tried to alleviate her suffering by giving her extra provisions, and by assuring her that his love was not based on her ability to have children. Nevertheless, she still struggled, and there wasn't much he could do to alleviate that; she had to deal with her pain herself.

It isn't easy to see someone you care about having a hard time, is it? My mother's health failed first, and she eventually needed to reside in a care facility. I remember many times Dad and I would go to spend time with her or to take her with us somewhere, and each time when we left her again, he would shake his head and say, "Poor thing." It was just hard to see a once active and vibrant woman decline so dramatically. Whether you care for a person with a disabling physical or mental illness, or are helping someone who is declining with old age, it is the kind of experience that can tug at your heartstrings. There are things you can do to help alleviate their suffering. You already know what many of them are: flowers on the bedside, a big smile with kind words, making a favorite dish or taking a drive on a sunny day. But you cannot take all the hardship away. Nor are you meant to do so.

You can only do so much; the rest is what the other person has to face in life themselves. You support them, encourage them, help them...but still, their struggle is their own. After all, you know that you have struggles you have to face on your own and that no one else can do that for *you*, either.

In Hannah's case, the struggle ended when God answered her prayer and gave her a son she named Samuel, "God heard." The story's happy ending was that her son became one of Israel's greatest leaders. But not all stories of struggle end so easily or happily. Some struggles only end at the gates of heaven.

So, though it is hard to watch one you care about struggle with the hard things of their lives, the sad fact is that it is part of this fallen world. And it is something God can use in lots of ways, hard though it may be. With you there, and God as well, the person you care for doesn't have to face the struggle all alone. And sometimes, in struggles, not having to face them alone is what helps most of all.

MY PRAYER FOR YOU THIS WEEK

My prayer this week is that you will discover a deepening of the relationship you experience with the one you love, and in your relationship with God as well. As you share your heart and love with this special person in very tangible ways, may God open your heart to receive the love they have for you and that God has for you as well. Amen.

Day 36 Matthew 6:19-21

Jesus tells us not to get caught up gathering our treasures here on earth, treasures which are all perishable.

Instead, we are to store up our treasure in heaven. That is a high sounding principle, but it can be very hard as our lives get so cluttered with the rat race, or with stuff, or just keeping up with the monthly bills. In fact, we can get so busy with those kinds of things, that we forget to make sacred time in our lives with God.

The challenge Jesus gives us is to change our perspective enough that our awareness, our investment, our hearts will be prioritized according to the values of heaven, rather than the corruptible values and pressures of earth. I was struck by this a few days ago, when I was walking to the auto mechanic's shop to pick up my car. I happened to walk through neighborhoods from my childhood. I passed by the home where I grew up, my elementary school, old neighborhood grocery stores, the homes where friends and I played together and the places where I used to climb trees. Two trees that I especially remember were gone, cut down long ago. Neglected homes were in disrepair. Neighborhood grocery stores have been converted to homes or torn down leaving only vacant lots. My elementary school is used for something else, the old playground now long gone. The fishpond next door to my home has been filled in. And the old home place is rather dilapidated, I'm sorry to say. If I needed graphic reminders that things here on earth don't last and aren't the best long term investment of our time and energy, I could have had none better than that walk.

On the other hand, each act of kindness, each time we forgive, each temptation we resist, each time we share our faith or pray...these are just a few of the things that get our hearts where they need to be. Caregiving is the great way to perfect these kinds of heart attitudes and priorities. These deeds, and so many others done in obedience to scripture as we seek to allow God to shape and use us, are the ways we build up our heavenly accounts. So as you do all these simple, mundane, and sometimes very tedious tasks of caregiving, realize that these are the ways you are making deposits in heaven, where your real riches will never fade. How are your daily deposits going?

Day 37 Luke 15:11-32

In a time when an individual comes to need caregiving, often the family will come together to decide as a family some of the key issues. That togetherness can be a great thing, and it is well worth cultivating because there may be times that group process will help you through some difficult times and tough decisions. On the other hand, it may be that in your situation as a caregiver there are other family members who could do a lot to help out, but don't. Today's passage has variously been called the parable of: "The Prodigal Son," "The Loving Father," and sometimes, "The Lost Son." (I prefer the last two titles myself.) Most of the time people focus on the younger brother, especially on the moment of his repentance and restoration. Sometimes they focus on the anger of the older brother, and the moment his father tries to help him understand the value of repentance. But caregivers might notice other things.

For instance, the young brother got his share of the possessions and then hit the road for a high time as a world traveler. So guess who was left to stay home and take care of dad? Yup. The caregiver brother! In his case, it was a role kind of dumped on him, although I suppose he could have left if he really wanted to...though that wasn't usual in the culture. He had stuck with his father, done the hard things day in and day out, and then resented it when the younger brother came back and received such an extravagant welcome.

He had forgotten some things. He forgot that he chose to stay around. He forgot that his dad noticed and appreciated what he did on a daily basis. He forgot that good fathers always love all their children, no matter how they behave. And he forgot that everything had already been divided, and the share of what was there as his father's now, was technically in the long run, his. He forgot how important the work he did was, when he thought nobody noticed. Maybe he forgot that he was really doing it for his father, and for God, not for recognition. Most of all, he had forgotten what a privilege it was to help his father and to spend time with him on a daily basis.

Those are some of the things he forgot. With all the responsibilities that you carry day by day, is there anything you have forgotten? We'll talk about this son some more, tomorrow. In the meantime, maybe you and God could just visit together about your situation.

Day 38   Luke 15:11-32

So, today we return to the story of the brothers and their father. The younger brother had chosen to return home and the older brother was upset with the result. He lashed out. Clearly there was some resentment over a variety of things, one of which is mentioned when he said that he had been slaving away for his dad over the years and has had no reward for his labors. While the younger brother enjoyed the "choice" to leave and the "choice" to come back, the older brother was stuck on the farm. Having his sibling come walking in made for a pretty awkward moment.

There have been times I have dealt with some of that. Haven't you had those times, too? Like when the one I care for has gone into the hospital and the family members at a distance want me to keep them informed as they try to decide whether or not they should come. In such times, it is hard to know exactly how to aid them. Such family members may not realize the luxury they have in being able to decide whether or not to come. I'm the caregiver; I just automatically have to go...no choice involved. Well, no reasonable choice, anyway (because I had made the choice long before to take on the role of caregiver).

Dealing with all the family members, one can start to feel like the older brother, resenting the lack of choice. Or if a relative comes who likes to take over (*which I have not had to deal with, thankfully*), the older brother's view of "I have been here doing this all along" can surface. Sometimes it surfaces in a humorous way (*I can't believe they are giving me advice on that, I handle that issue all the time!*), or sometimes not so humorous (*I already had things set up and worked through the problems and now they are moving backwards five steps instead of just asking first!*). Knowing how to respond can sometimes be tricky.

If you have times that you feel like the older brother with occasional resentments, let me offer a few suggestions. For example, you may not feel that you have the luxury of choosing that the other family members do. But remember, you also don't have the struggle of having to decide whether to risk spending time and money to come unnecessarily in a false emergency or to risk missing a last opportunity because you didn't come! You made the decision a long time ago as a blanket decision, so you don't wrestle with it every single time.

You may feel as though you have been there while they have not, and so you may resent intrusions or the lack of appreciation for your work. However, as the father told the older son, you and your charge could do special things any time you want, while the person at a distance only gets occasional opportunities. And, as least as far as *I* am concerned, I have tons of memorable relationship moments week after week which would not be my experience if I were at a distance instead of being caregiver.

The resentment and attitude of the older brother can be a real temptation when you are a caregiver. But it is just that: a temptation. Resist it and instead, find things to be thankful for in the opportunities you *do have*, rather than things to resent in the opportunities you *don't*.

Day 39 Psalm 119:9-10, 105

Sometimes when I wake up, I feel as if my whole day has already been consumed before I even head to the breakfast table! That happens because of all the things I know are on the schedule in the day's plan of caregiving. And of course, that does not include all the things that will pop up that aren't on the planned schedule. The question always is, of course, how to determine which things actually need to be done and which things I need to just let go or postpone when I am not able to get it all done.

In the midst of the hectic and stressful days of caregiving, when it feels as though there is no time to squeeze in anything else, it becomes even more important to make time for scripture. More than anything else, it is the quickest way for direct access to guidance from God. And when you have on your plate lots of responsibility and more to do than can possibly be done, guidance in making wise use of each moment is pretty valuable. Did you read today's passage carefully? Did you notice what difference the scripture can make in your life?

I know that spending time in the scriptures can easily get shoved aside when you are feeling pressed for time. I know it all too well. But choosing to fight the inclination to do that something else and making a few moments to at least read a Psalm or two, will pay big dividends. God's desire is to help you handle that crazy schedule with all the demands on your time. Besides, it may well be that the experience of feeling trapped by those demands could be the way God is guiding your choices, and that you will only realize this truth as you open your heart to His voice in the scriptures. Not only does time spent meditating on God's word build your relationship and connection with God and provide the spiritual and emotional strength for each day, it is the primary means by which God brings guidance into our lives. Taking time to read from your Bible will create an opportunity for God to speak to you to shape or affirm your plans for the day, and it may help you realize that some things just aren't that important. After all, the best plans you will ever make for any day, are plans to follow the guidance of God.

Day 40 Romans 8:18

Is the one you care for suffering? When my mother had Alzheimer's, one of the biggest blessings for those of us who cared for her (and it was also a blessing for her, she just didn't realize it), was that because of all she didn't understand and remember, she didn't remember or focus on the pain she was experiencing in her body from her various illnesses. She had already had plenty of years that included some painful suffering, due to problems with her knees and shoulders especially. It would have been very hard for her to accept some of the changes life had brought her way, but with her memory impaired, she was not bothered by them because she didn't fully comprehend what had happened. In fact, it is probably the case that my father suffered more as Mom lost her memory and ability to communicate, and as he saw her decline physically.

I have known other individuals who suffered terribly as they declined. Some of them suffered ravaging diseases that were painful and devastating. Other times, the anguish I observed was mental, as stroke or other illness left limited physical ability for a person whose mind was still very coherent, but trapped inside his or her body. Suffering can come in a variety of forms.   In any case, it is a hard thing to watch the decline as you care for another person day by day.

Paul also suffered, but in a different way. In fact, some of the things he suffered were awful...beatings and unjust imprisonments for example. So when he makes the statement that he does here in Romans, he is speaking from experience. If you could catch just a bit of his perspective, it may just transform everything for you: *the suffering you see is not even worth comparing to the incredible glory we shall one day experience when we see Jesus, face to face.* Absolutely no comparison. So much so that it isn't even worth *trying* to compare this world's suffering with the glory of God! Sometimes, that can be hard to remember here on earth, but it is true nonetheless. There are times we simply need to stop what we are doing, turn our attention away from the hard things we face, and remind ourselves of this incredible truth.

Day 41   Acts 3:18-20

I like the phrase used in this passage: "times of refreshing...from the presence of the Lord." The promised "times of refreshing" Peter referred to in his sermon come because of the fact that Jesus fulfilled the messianic prophecies, providing the long sought after forgiveness for sin for any who would take it. When we turn from our sinful ways, God comes to us bringing true refreshment: the burdens of guilt and heartache caused by our sin find themselves banished out of the presence of our gracious and forgiving God, as we are granted a fresh start.

I just like that word, "refreshing." Just the word itself arouses images of freshness, exuberance, life and sunshine. It makes me think of an ice-cold lemonade on a sultry summer day. Or, these days, I think of the difference between a battery about to die and that same battery operating a device at full speed after the battery was

refreshed by a night plugged into a charger. Energy.
Revitalization. Release of stress and uncertainty. Ready to
take on the world. Refreshed!

I know that many times when I served as a caregiver,
the idea of such refreshing was like a mirage on the
horizon. I longed for it, but was too worn out to pursue or
too overscheduled to have time for the activities that
promise refreshing. But God's promise of refreshing times
isn't based on our schedules, but on His power and
activity...*God sends* times of refreshing, we don't have to
manufacture them.

Are you hungry for such a time right now? If you are
feeling ragged and worn, or if you have been falling short
of what you would like to be, then perhaps today would be
a good day to take a minute to turn to God, asking Him to
surround you with His refreshing presence! It doesn't
require a trip to the beach, or even a weekend getaway,
nice as those might be. God's refreshing can come to your
soul through even brief times spent before Him. You may
want to go sit in a church sanctuary in quiet reflection. Or
soft music and prayer while sitting in your car in the
hospital parking lot may be your refuge. An open Bible
with a cup of coffee is the preference of others. Times of
refreshing can come in a variety of ways and the briefest
stretches of time. Like those who turned aside from their
day's activities to listen to what Peter had to say, I
encourage you to turn aside today for even a few moments
of refreshment with God.

Day 42 Psalm 115:9-13

It is unusual in scripture for something to be repeated
three times. You frequently see a double repetition, for
repetition is one of the poetic styles used throughout the
Psalms and other biblical poetry. But when lines are
repeated more than that, it is worth noticing. And in the

middle of this Psalm, we run across one such occurrence. Ask yourself, "What is important enough about this teaching that this threefold repetition is used here, instead of two?"

One of the things I like about this repetition is the way the descriptive circles include various groups of people. The description given of God in this passage is first applied to Israel, the chosen people of God. The next step is to highlight the house of Aaron...the family of priests. I think it is kind of interesting that the priests are listed second, not first. It implies to me that God desires to be a God of all the people, not just some special group of ministers who somehow are more holy or have some kind of corner on the "God market." On the other hand, it also indicates that those in ministry have just as much need for God to be their help and shield as anybody else!

But then, the last circle indicates that the list does not *exclude* other; rather, these circles are intended to *include* anyone who believes, regardless of location, regardless of heritage. The circle of promise is addressed to "you who fear the Lord." It includes you and it includes me as we walk in proper fear of the Lord. So what is the threefold promise?

God is described as a God Who helps, as our source of help. Of course, that is only relevant to people who *need* help. But then, the reality is that we *all* need help in one way or another, at one time or another. And when it comes to mercy and forgiveness of sins, we *absolutely* all need God's help, for without it we would have no chance before a holy God. I am sure you can identify some ways that you could use some help right now in your life, can't you? Yes, God identifies Himself as the God Who helps, in contrast to the idols mentioned earlier in the Psalm who cannot even help themselves!

Also, God as a shield is an interesting characteristic to highlight three times, isn't it? It is especially so for those who live in cultures or neighborhoods where daily there are life- threatening experiences close at hand. When at risk of assault and attack, a shield is exactly the kind of thing one would need. And spiritually, those of us who are believers are under attack constantly, for Satan longs to undermine your faith. Only the shield of God is capable of protecting us from all spiritual attacks.

So included with these precious promises of God there is the key instruction, which is also repeated three times, to *trust God*. The Bible doesn't underscore things more than that. If you need help, if you need a shield, whatever your needs in life...***trust God***.

MY PRAYER FOR YOU THIS WEEK

My prayer this week is for you to experience moments of joy each and every day. May God bring a smile to your face through scenes of beauty, laughter to your lips through a well-timed joke or a silly shared memory, or maybe even a laugh at yourself over a foolish faux pas. And most of all, may you be reminded of the joy of knowing that God's love and salvation are yours. Amen.

Day 43 Matthew 22:35-40 and 2 Timothy 3:1-5

Some people are really good at loving their neighbor, and would go to any lengths to help out somebody in need. But they are not so good at loving themselves, because it feels very selfish to them. In fact, the passage in Timothy gives a stern warning about those who become "lovers of self." How does one square the notion of loving a neighbor as your own self with being warned that love of self is a dangerous thing?

I believe the answer is multifaceted. First is the notion that we are to love our neighbors to the same degree that we would be caring for ourselves, to treat others no differently than how we would treat ourselves in the same situation. The second facet, and perhaps just as important, is the fact that 2 Timothy makes no indication that the person mentioned loves anybody BUT himself! That is, the image Jesus presents is to love others as yourself, not excluding one or the other, nor treating one as less important than the other. While it may seem noble to love other people and denigrate oneself, that is *not* the teaching of scripture. We can choose to put the interests of others ahead of our own and even lay down our lives for somebody else, but that does not mean we don't love the self God has created us to be. Instead, that may actually be loving self in one of the highest degrees, because by laying ourselves aside for another, we choose to love ourselves enough to be the very best kind of person we could be.

Now, I said all these things so that I could get to my main point. While you are caring for another, it is not selfish, self-centered or wrong to also care for yourself. Your love for that other person is a spiritual outpouring of your love of self, demonstrated by being the kind of person God has designed you to be, living the kind of life you know would be pleasing to God and fulfilling for yourself.   To carelessly throw yourself aside and ignore your own needs is to neglect the gift God has placed within you and abuse the creation of God. Both facets are important. But there is an even more practical issue at hand.

If you wear yourself out caring for your charge to the point that you have nothing left to give, who will care for the person after you no longer can? Or, if you wear yourself completely out at this point in the process, what will you do if you are needed even more later on? To be able to effectively provide loving care to this person in need, you also have to balance it with the love and care needed for yourself. Balance is the important word.

Loving yourself in an appropriate balance enables you to love effectively in the caregiving role. Without it, you can become resentful, irritable, exhausted, ill, or in some cases, so weak you will not be able to continue the work. The hard part is when you realize that in order to be able to continue caregiving in love, you may have to allow others to assist you, or even take over tasks for you in the form of in-home or in-facility care. Never forget that caring for others is closely bound up with caring for self. It will make you a better caregiver.

Day 44 Hebrews 11:8-9

If you have committed yourself to caregiving, then there are a whole bunch of other things you are *not* able to commit yourself to doing. Some of them are very good things, such as service clubs or acting as a group leader at your church, or maybe even committing to family vacation time! Some things may not be terribly important, like not being able to attend your favorite annual festival, or to spend the amount of time you would like doing the gardening. Others might be pretty important things. You may have to put your career on hold to do what you are doing, or you may have had to limit your involvement in the activities of your children or grandchildren, activities you would have otherwise enjoyed doing.

The cost of providing caregiving is not measured merely in dollars and cents, but also in terms of opportunities left aside and priorities exchanged.   Many of the choices made by caregivers go contrary to the world's definition of success. Perhaps you have known some people, as I have, who would say to you, "Why don't you just put that person in some kind of care facility? Why do you try to do it all yourself?" You don't need me to answer that, do you? Only people who don't do what you are doing need to be told the answers to those questions.

You, it seems to me, are more like Abraham as described in this verse in Hebrews: if you wanted success the way the world views success, then you would be changing your priorities and choosing other opportunities to get there. Instead, you have a higher calling, and following that calling means your treasure is a heavenly one, rather than treasures valued by the world. Somehow I think you are making the wiser choice.

Day 45 Ruth 1:14-18

Ruth made an intentional decision to stay with her mother-in-law, Naomi. Naomi tried to talk her out of it. She had warned Ruth that going with Naomi could ruin Ruth's future, especially her chances of finding a husband. The family obligation requiring a man to marry the widow of his deceased brother was not going to be an option; Naomi had no other sons, and odds are would not have sons again.

But Ruth knew that Naomi needed her support and help, so Ruth consciously decided to let her own life take a backseat to meeting the needs of her mother-in-law. There have been lots of speculations about the various reasons Ruth would do that, including her longing to know better the God she had learned of through Naomi's teachings and example. The various speculations probably contain tidbits of truth with regard to Ruth's motivations. But I believe the scripture clearly suggests that one of the core reasons for Ruth's choice was that Naomi really needed her, and Ruth was the kind of person to stick with a loved one in need.

This may sound a lot like your life, too, these days. The outcome of this story is probably best summed up by the words of Jesus in Matthew 16:25, where He said that those who lose their lives will find it (though He refers specifically to losing one's life for Jesus' sake). It sure happened for Ruth. We don't know exactly how much faith played into Ruth's decision, but she truly did end up finding her life. Ruth put her future at risk when she followed Naomi, and ended up blessed when she found a husband in Boaz, the man who would take care of both her and Naomi from then on. And Ruth was also blessed when she found herself placed squarely into the genealogy of King David and of Jesus Himself!

Like Ruth, you may feel as though your work as a caregiver has placed your future at risk. But know that God holds your future, just as surely as He did Ruth's, and He will honor the choices you are making as you lay down your life for another. After all, isn't that what He did for us?

Day 46 Luke 12:13-21

I remember once being called by the director of the local funeral home to come visit with a family in preparation for a funeral, since the family didn't attend church or know a pastor to conduct the service. As I slipped in the back door of the funeral home, the director pulled me aside and quietly said to me, "I should warn you about what you are about to get into. The body isn't even cold, and they are already in there fighting about who is going to get everything." He then wished me luck, pointed me toward the room and disappeared into those mysterious caverns of offices that all funeral homes seem to have. It turned out to be quite the experience!

In the midst of caregiving, you may have those times when you find yourself focused on the needs of the person while some other family members are more concerned about the stuff, things like finances and heirlooms. They may even accuse you of manipulating things for personal gain. (Which means by the way, that, as a believer, you really need to do your very best to operate with honesty, transparency and integrity.) In fact, some may even start staking claims and marking out territory. It can be very difficult for you, and also for the one you love.

In today's story, a man came to Jesus asking Him to make his brother divide the estate with him. Jesus declined the role of arbiter, perhaps because He knew that was something the two of them needed to work out for themselves, perhaps because He believed they were focusing on the wrong priorities, or perhaps because He simply knew better than to insert Himself into a family squabble!

I will only make a couple of suggestions for you, as I mainly wanted to acknowledge the existence of this tough topic, and encourage you to find ways to face it responsibly. The first suggestion is merely to not let yourself lose the focus of what is truly important in the ministry of caregiving. Your calling is to help make life for your loved one better, and to remember that the true treasures are not here on earth. The other suggestion I will offer is for you to have open discussions with your loved one and/or arrange opportunities for meetings to learn about living wills, planned giving, living trusts or funeral planning...the essential end of life issues. Near the end of his life, my dad even took time to make a distribution list of various household items, too, based on conversations he had with various family members as well as tasks that were a priority for him. These things were all very helpful after he had gone home to the Lord, serving as written guides of his wishes in these areas and thus avoiding the nasty disputes that can often happen.

As caregiver, these may be difficult topics to raise. But you will do your loved one and the family a great service if you are willing to be the one who helps him or her prepare answers to the questions that will need to be faced. You certainly should include other family members appropriately, and don't be afraid to seek out individuals in the community who have the expertise to help guide the process. You may end up preserving family harmony that might have otherwise been lost, and will certainly help make the critical end of life and funeral details all go a bit more smoothly.

Day 47 Isaiah 43:1-2

There is no promise from God saying that being a Christian means you will never have difficult times or experience extreme hardships. Nor does it mean that things won't come into your life that can make you feel overwhelmed. Like I need to tell *you* that, right? Then again, maybe I do. I think every caregiver can identify plenty of times when it just becomes hard and they feel overwhelmed, causing them to wonder why God doesn't seem to be helping. Well, God may not prevent hardships from coming in our lives, but there are things He *has* promised.

Some of those promises are presented in today's passage, which is one of my favorites. The promise is that when things get really hard, you won't be alone because He will be with you. The promise is that though the storms may rage around you, creating conditions that feel like a flood that could sweep you away, either they will be limited or you will be protected in such a way that you won't be overwhelmed and carried off. The promise is that the fires may rage, but you won't be burned. There are even more promises within this passage. The promise that God knows you by name! The promise that He has redeemed you, and will keep you forever his.

Spend some time rereading today's passage slowly, phrase by phrase. Absorb the promises made to you. Revel in the assurance of His protection. (Perhaps you may want to review again the promises listed in Appendix One.) Let the fears for the worst subside, knowing that the One Who is best is always at your side. Always.

Day 48   Judges 13:2-5, 24-25

Some of the readers of this book are in a uniquely different and difficult situation than the rest. Some of you are caregivers who feel bound to your obligation for the rest of your life, rather than the rest of the life of the one for whom you are caring. This can be because you have a child who has a severe illness or disability of some sort. It can be because the disability occurred to your spouse early in your married life, and you both have many years ahead of you.

This challenge can appear as daunting and noble, but can also be experienced as never-ending and hopeless. When you feel this way, sometimes a sense of guilt is associated with those feelings because of the belief that if you truly loved the individual, then you shouldn't worry about how long you will have to provide care. The realization that your entire life is going to be centered around caring for this individual rather than other possibilities you may have dreamed of for your life, can be a difficult thing to face.

I have known some who cared for a disabled child, believing they were obligated to keep that child at home as the only way to care for him or her. Sometimes, it truly is the best. Sometimes, though, the parent realized their child would have more opportunities and higher quality care at facilities designed to meet their needs; things like group homes come to mind. Others kept their child at home until the disease had run its course and their child died. That is truly a heart-wrenching experience. In any such cases, it helps for the caregiver to have a sense that they truly did the best they could, and that they were doing what they truly believed was best for their charge. It is one of those decisions that only the people involved can make, and it is certainly not my place to second guess the choices they make.

With all the stress involved in this kind of caregiving, there are some, sadly, who cannot endure. A spouse wants out, so leaves to find what they hope is an easier life with somebody else who does not have such disabilities. Occasionally a parent may leave spouse and child with the result that the spouse left behind is abandoned to care for the child alone. The fact that this kind of thing happens is indicative of just how difficult the challenge truly can be.

When Samson's mother was told by the angel that she would have a child, she was also told that he was to be a Nazirite from birth, which was a special kind of committed life before God. The story is very unusual, but I simply want to focus on the fact that, from birth, Samson was called into a unique and special life of service to God. (Reading the rest of Samson's life story, one wonders if he ever really understood the obligation!)

It is entirely possible that you have been called in a similar manner, for a specific kind of lifelong service. All caregivers are called that way for a time, I believe, but some have been entrusted with the more challenging task of a caregiving for a lifetime. It can be a difficult and lonely calling. The measure of success will not be in the public eye, but in the private experiences of a disabled person who was loved well in life.

If God has entrusted you with such a calling, let me highlight for you a couple of things in closing. First, God doesn't entrust such individuals to just anybody. As I have indicated before, He must see something very special about you to call you to such a life of service, to select *you* to care for one of His creatures who is unable to care for him or herself. And second, if God has truly called you to this ministry, then the only way to fulfill it successfully is to call out to God for the strength, wisdom and help you will need. It does *not* mean you have to do it alone; God may have an abundance of helpers available for you, or you may be the primary (or even the sole) caregiver. Trust Him to provide according to your need and ability, but also in accordance with His wisdom and purpose...even if you cannot see that purpose. May God's special blessing rest on those of you in this unique and challenging calling. You have my admiration.

Day 49 Mark 5:21-27

Jesus was kind of a walking emergency room, wasn't he? There He was, walking along, and then all of a sudden, there was this urgent demand to come and see a dying boy. So off He went. And then as He was walking toward *that* emergency, He gets interrupted again by a woman seeking help. I don't know what was else on His schedule that day, but Jesus had an amazing ability to adapt His plans to the needs of those around him, even at a moment's notice. Emergency situations almost seemed to be His specialty!

Most of us caregivers know our way around the hospitals and emergency rooms pretty well, don't we? In fact, much of my book writing has taken place in hospitals and doctors' offices, while waiting for medical techs to determine and administer treatments. I am actually in the ER right now, waiting for test results with the one I care for, having just brought him in not long ago. I had a pretty full day of plans that I had to drop today, and often do when I have had to come out here. Some of those things *have* to be done today, so I will have to grab a few seconds when I can to go do them. Some I can bring with me, such as writing.

But others will just have to wait until another day, because they are less important than what I am doing now. I, too, have to adapt.

Many of the things we experience as interruptions and diversions were interpreted by Jesus during His life as the opportunities sent to Him by God. He saw these things as part of the way God guided His ministry. Instead of calling them problems, He considered them to be the opportunities He used for God's glory. I suspect your life schedule gets upset from time to time (or maybe minute by minute!). I wonder if you are able, as Jesus did, to see the changes as one of the ways God guides us to opportunities. I admit, it is sometimes a tough perspective to get, but once achieved, it sure helps!

MY PRAYER FOR YOU THIS WEEK

My prayer this week is that you will have an uncanny sensitivity to the heart and desires of the one you care for, aware of the needs both spoken and unspoken. And that the sensitivity you have will extend to an awareness of the leading of the Spirit of God so that, in every task, you fulfill the purpose of God. Amen.

Day 50   Joshua 14:10-13

There is a delicate balance that exists in the ministry of caregiving. That balance is between doing what is necessary to help make life better for the ones in our care, and being careful to not do the things that would be best done by the individual themselves (which might be best for a variety of reasons). It is much more difficult to identify that boundary than one might think, isn't it?

For example, if we do too much, including things they could do for themselves, we risk taking away their dignity.

They begin to feel useless and unneeded. If we only allow them to do what they are *sure* they can do, we invite complacency and maybe more dependency than is needed. By leaving challenges to them, there is opportunity for growth, recovery and accomplishment. Yet leaving too big a challenge results in discouragement and hopelessness. Kind of tough to figure out, isn't it?

The perfect example we find in scripture is this wonderful story of Caleb. You may recall he was one of only two spies Moses sent ahead into the Promised Land who came back with a positive report. As a result, he was also one of the only two spies who actually got to enter the new homeland. As they were settling the land, Caleb was eighty-five years old, an aged warrior, ready for the rest home, right? Well, he *was* 85. But as for the rest home, he came to Joshua seeking the land that contained giants, the land that would be the hardest to capture. *In his old age, Caleb yearned for a fresh challenge!* And it was a good experience for him!

Dad always loved to plant a garden, and did till the very end, sometimes with help from young people we would hire to work with him on it. Mom always liked to feel like she was helping, and folding towels or cleaning the table were here specialties. As you care for the person in your charge, don't ever underestimate their ability to face new challenges, whether they are young with a disability or elderly with a wheelchair. Wisely allow your loved ones the freedom to explore new possibilities for their lives.

Day 51 Isaiah 40:31

This has always been one of my very favorite verses, and I think one of the most relevant in the midst of caregiving. Weary. In need of renewal. Searching for strength. Feeling so rushed that there seems to be not time to just stop and rejuvenate. Sound familiar?

Into that context the words of Isaiah boom forth. "Wait for the Lord!" Tarry in His presence. Don't let yourself get ahead of him. Be still and allow God to speak, to guide, to strengthen, to invigorate, to heal, to refresh, to give you the wings that will enable you to fly like an eagle and the strength to feel again the vigor of youth. These instructions are critical in times like these. In order to renew your strength, wait for the Lord.

That's all I have to say today. In many ways, it is all that needs to be said. It is up to you and me to each find ways to make some time to simply wait in the presence of God for his new strength to fill our lives.

Day 52 John 15:12-14

Jesus, of course, was primarily talking about His own sacrificial death when He talked about laying down His life for His friends. It always reminds me of war stories I have heard in which individuals saved others by risking or even giving up their own lives. My grade school principal had a prosthetic arm because in World War II, he somehow took the explosion of a grenade in order to protect the others in his platoon. Recently, my dad was awarded a bronze star sixty years after World War II, because he and another man risked their lives to return, several times and under fire, into the field of battle at Monte Casino to rescue New Zealand soldiers who lay wounded and dying.

Incidents like these where someone risks or gives one's life in the defense of others are generally recognized as acts of great sacrifice. But, heroic and incredible as they are, they often are one-time events that happen within a matter of hours. As a caregiver, you also are laying down your life, on a daily basis, perhaps for a very long time. There are vacations you may not be able to take. There may be financial burdens resulting from the extended situation. Your emotions may be stretched to their limit, and you may be so fatigued you have energy for nothing else. Your life becomes consumed with all the responsibilities, and your thoughts, on the back burner if not in the forefront of your mind, are constantly dwelling on balancing your needs with those of the one in your care. And you may find, as I have, that you don't even realize the extent to which your life is wrapped up in caregiving until the day comes when he or she has passed away and you no longer have that responsibility. At that time, the void left behind is staggering, and you may realize as I have just how much time, energy and life you have invested in the task of caregiving.

Hear, today, the words of Jesus to you: "There is no greater love."

Day 53 Matthew 6:34

There simply aren't enough hours in a day, are there? Actually, yes there are. What there isn't, is enough time to do all the *other* things that don't really need to be done today, because they don't belong to today. Jesus said that each day's load is sufficient for that one day, and that wisdom would tell us to leave tomorrow's struggles for tomorrow.

Easier said than done, huh? At least, I certainly have my share of sleepless nights and wee hour awakenings with concerns, worries, fears and thoughts plaguing my mind. In fact, some days, I wake up and feel hours behind because of all the things I believe I have to accomplish that day.

But I don't.

I don't have to accomplish *everything* in that one, single day.   There are concerns that *have* to be handled in a given day. And there are concerns *demanding* to be cared for that day, whether they need to be or not. In times when I feel overwhelmed, I am not always able to discern the difference. But some days, I (and you!) just have to let some things go, because they don't really matter. Or even if they do matter, they may not have to be done *today*. God's design is for us to only do one day's tasks in a day. The rest can wait till tomorrow. Or next week. Or maybe it doesn't really matter if they *never* get done. What matters is that I do today's tasks, today.

Day 54 Philippians 1:22-25

I had to make some decisions over the last few weeks, myself. Such as, do you want him transferred to a bigger hospital? If the situation turns bad, what measures do you want us to take and not to take? Should we transfer him to another kind of rehab facility now, or wait a few more weeks? I really don't need to list for you all my questions; they are the same kind of questions as the ones you have probably had to face, or one day will.

In some cases, those decisions are less difficult to make because you have guidance from a living will or conversations you have had with your loved one long ago. But even then, I would comment that helpful as these things are when making decisions, the emotional impact of it all can still be very strong on you. I remember words of decision coming out of my mouth, voicing the guidance I had been given years before, but as I heard them out loud, it felt like signing somebody's death warrant. It was hard to walk away.

One recent decision was apparently a real toss up, advantages and disadvantages   whichever way I decided. Perhaps that was what Paul felt like as he wrestled with life decisions, too. There were family members I could consult with, but they were not on the scene with all the observations you get first hand and time was of the essence. Ultimately, it was my decision to make, so I made the best judgment I could make based on the information I had or could get, and based on the reality of how things were *that day.*

Sometimes, the path is not so clear. Sometimes we are in situations much like Paul's, where we could go one way or the other, and we have to choose. We know our choices may result in consequences we had not foreseen. It is the reality of life, the reality of caregiving. Gather your information, seek appropriate counsel, ask God for wisdom, then make your choice and give the consequences to God. Then walk away, knowing you did the best you know how to do in the situation with the knowledge you had at the time.

Day 55 Galatians 6:8-10

Don't grow weary in the doing of good? And the last half of verse nine challenges us not to give up or lose heart. Are you kidding me? I am convinced that the work of caregiving is a good thing, aren't you? But it is absolutely a very wearing thing to do, right? It is an experience in which it can be easy to grow weary and discouraged, to "lose heart" and just want to give up. But Paul just tells us not to grow weary, as if we just decide we aren't going to do so. It seems to me that this is one of those verses that would elicit the response, "Easier said than done!" Know what I mean?

In caregiving, many of us spend a great deal of our time feeling weary...very weary...because it is such a drain in so many ways. It can be draining physically, if you are running hither and yon trying to meet all the needs, or if your role includes a lot of "manhandling" to assist your charge with showers, dressing and so forth. It can be draining emotionally, as you repeat the same instructions time and again, or endure unfair abuse, or struggle with sorrow over the decline of one you love. It can be draining financially, as resources dissipate when expenses mount, or your own work schedule suffers due to the shift in priorities. No wonder so many caregivers look and feel so weary!

But Paul tells us not to grow weary, not to lose heart in our doing good. So if on the one hand we believe that caregiving is a good thing, and on the other hand believe Paul when he tells us not to grow weary even though it is a taxing experience, how in the world does this make any sense? Can we really just choose not to be weary, not to lose heart?

I would suggest a possible answer. I believe Paul bothers to write this down specifically *because* doing these kinds of good things *can* wear you out. He knows, probably by his own experience, that one can get discouraged, lose heart, and grow weary of trying. His wording is intended as encouragement for those very times. It is the equivalent of the modern phrase, "Hang in there." And as so often is the case, the encouragement comes from taking a long view. There is recognition that your efforts are but for a time and assurance that there is a good reward in the long run, at the appropriate time or, as Paul puts it, "in due season."

So on the days you feel like giving up, just don't. Hang in there. Find a way to get as much of the needed rest, help and support as you can. See the job through, making appropriate adjustments along the way. Trust that the future is in God's hands and know that when all is said and done, it will be well worth your while.

Day 56 Revelation 21:1-4

Caregiving brings a person very near to the world of suffering and sickness here in this world. We see firsthand the ravages of disease, physical infirmities and the suffering associated with them, or with old age. We seek medical help because we don't want life to be that way, as if we inherently sense that this is not the ideal life. And the scriptures teach that, indeed, it isn't the way things ought to be. Rather, it is this way temporarily in a fallen world infected by sin. But not forever.

In old age, the promise from Revelation that all things will be made new is a mind-boggling promise. In times of sickness or suffering, the promise that they shall be banished forever is a dream beyond hope. When the tears of this life have wet our cheeks far too often as we watched the struggle of those we love, the promise that every tear shall be wiped away for eternity is a comfort beyond imagination.

Whether hard to imagine or not, these are the promises God has made. And God has made them for *you!* In your darkest hour, in your greatest struggle, in the deepest burdens of your heart, hear the promise of God that, one day, He will make all things new and the difficulties of this life will be no more.

MY PRAYER FOR YOU THIS WEEK

My prayer for you this week is that God will give you the wisdom you need. Choices abound on a daily basis, some of which are very simple, others perhaps having life-changing results for you, for the one you love, and for extended family or friends. May the knowledge you gain of the situations you face be complemented by the wisdom to know how to use the knowledge in the best possible way. Amen.

Day 57 Psalm 90:10 and James 4:13-14

Life on earth is very brief. There are times when it feels too brief. Sometimes, though, when things are hard, it can feel as though life drags on forever. But it doesn't. Compared to eternity, our lives here are just a mere blink of an eye. Today's scriptures articulate that concept in such vivid terms for us.

The opportunity you have to serve as caregiver is also short-lived. For most of us, it is only for a season of our lives that we are filling this role. The person probably hasn't needed caregiving throughout your entire lifetime, and probably not the entire course of theirs, either (although there are exceptions). But for most of us caregivers, it is the need for now. Even if your situation is such that caregiving IS for a major portion of your life, even then, in light of eternity, it is only a brief moment on the stage of history.

With an eternal perspective, we can see this as a service opportunity for a time, an opportunity we won't have forever, a very brief segment of our eternal existence. It can be important to keep such a perspective, especially if you are having days that feel as if your task has dragged on for too long. This chapter of life will come to a close at some point; your task is simply to fulfill the calling God has for you now. Someday your life may shift to another chapter, but until then, choose to make this brief time a time well spent.

Day 58 Philippians 1:2-5

I have found in my experience of caregiving that along with the hardships and stress, there are also opportunities to intentionally create special memories and make choices that intersperse some incredibly *good* things in with the incredibly *hard* things that are part and parcel of caregiving responsibilities. I have made trips, watched movies, shared memories, recorded stories, joined in projects and enjoyed laughter with the ones I care for, and over time each of those moments has become a special memory.

There will come a time when the one you care for is gone, and you will be left with memories. Some of those memories will be bittersweet memories that cause you to feel the loss. Some will be memories that bring a deep sense of satisfaction, as you reflect on all the ways you worked hard to make sure that things went well for your loved one. Some memories will bring a tinge of regret, because of things like the day you chose not to sit and visit, or the request you were unable to fulfill. If you make wise choices along the way, there will be memories you will treasure that will continue to grow sweeter over time. Special memories of times together that only you and your loved one shared: times full of joy, special activities, and precious conversation. One day you will join Paul as you give thanks with every remembrance of those you love.

Though your time may be under great constraints, do not let the constraints prevent you from planting seeds of memories that will yield a wonderful harvest of joy for many years to come. Follow the impulse that causes you to make that sudden jaunt to the old home place, or take your loved one with you on the run to the lumber yard. An ice cream run for sundaes and lemonade can cool a hot summer day and bring smiles to a tired face. Since we can't always predict which events will become the most meaningful memories in the future, it is always a good idea to over plant so as to reap a bumper crop!

Day 59 Judges 3:7-11

In the history of biblical Israel, there were many times the nation would be struggling for various reasons, usually because of the attacks of enemies. The people would experience difficult times, until the time came when God would raise up a deliverer and rescue the people. Then the summary would include the phrase that "the land had rest." That peaceful time would last until the next period of struggle came, in many cases prompted again by their own poor choices.

That cycle is indicative of a lot of life, don't you think? Sometimes we struggle and sometimes life is easier. There simply are times we need someone to lift our burden. Sometimes the predicaments we experience are of our own creation. In some very real ways, the years dedicated to caregiving are years of struggle, albeit struggle with purpose. There are many things that would be easier if we didn't have that responsibility; but since we do, we work to juggle everything so as to make things work. As in the history of Israel, the struggle is but for a season; there will also be a time of rest. And sometimes knowing rest will one day come is the very hope that can keep you strong through the time of struggle.

In truth, part of what makes rest so "restful" is the fact that strenuous experiences wear us down and cause us to feel *in need* of rest. If every day was nothing but rest, we would probably not find it nearly as exhilarating or pleasurable. It would probably become extremely boring in short order (although as hectic as things have been, there are times I'd like to try it just to find out, wouldn't you?).

When you have been stretched to the limit, worked yourself into exhaustion, or endured to the point of fatigue, then a period of rest becomes heaven on earth. So take heart! A day will come when you will experience rest from your labors: God will send the deliverance you need *at the appropriate time*. And eventually we will enter into the eternal rest with God. Until those times come, try to grab a few catnaps along the way just to keep an even keel, okay?

Day 60 Lamentations 3:22-23

I like this passage. Actually, I like this whole book. For many people, this is the only part of Lamentations they have ever read or heard. That is kind of sad, because the strength of these verses rests in the context in which they were written. The context is that the writer is experiencing and commenting on the destruction of Jerusalem by the enemies of Israel. More than just a battle between countries, the downfall of Jerusalem and defeat of God's chosen people are experienced as a faith crisis when the Almighty God's protection seemed powerless against an enemy coming from a world filled with idols and false prophets. The people of Israel struggled for centuries with this destruction (and the later Roman destruction of the temple as well), searching for answers as to the role their lack of obedience played in the tragedy and what it meant that God would allow such things to happen.

It is one thing to talk about God's mercies being fresh day by day when the sun is shining and everything is going your way. It is another when you are in deep struggle and sorrow, and those mercies are needed to help you just get through the day. Depending on which translation you are using, verse 22 says that God's love never ceases or that His mercy keeps us from being consumed. Regardless of which way you translate it, in the context of the entire book these verses indicate a keen awareness that it is only God's mercy that kept the writer going day by day, an awareness that he was utterly dependent on God's mercy and love.

What keeps you going? What will get you through today? Tomorrow? God does not give us grace for the things we do not face in life. He only grants grace for what we *do* have to handle. He also does not give us the mercy and grace to make it through tomorrow; He grants it for each day as it comes. Though you may have been worn to a frazzle yesterday, and may be concerned about what may come tomorrow, look for God's love and mercy to be there for you *today*, in a fresh and vital way.

God's grace is enough to enable *you* to face whatever you have to deal with as well. Those things that are simply too tough to handle are the very opportunities in your life where you can let God's light to shine instead of your own. Whether you desperately want God to remove something from your life, or help you deal with the things that cannot be removed, God's grace is the one resource that will enable you to handle whatever life may bring. It is available from God, twenty four hours a day, seven days a week...you just have to ask for it.

Day 61 Luke 5:17-19

When I was young, I casually knew a boy who was a few years older than me, and who was bedfast because he had cerebral palsy. I remember a few times visiting at his house, though it was not often enough that my memories of the experience are vivid. I do remember that it was very awkward for me, as I didn't know how to communicate, and I didn't understand his illness, especially since I was so young. He died a teenager, and I can't say that I ever really *knew* him well, but he was an acquaintance. As an adult, I realize more about how tragic his illness was, and how difficult it must have been for his parents as they cared for him there in their home. He literally could not have made it without them.

This man on the bed in today's passage would never have been in Jesus' presence or received his healing had it not been for those who cared for him. In fact, as a friend of mine pointed out to me, it was *their* faith Jesus noticed as He proceeded to forgive and heal their companion. We don't know their relationship to him, only that they were acquaintances who cared about him in his plight. Individuals like this bedfast man and the young boy I knew, and perhaps the one you care for as well, depend on people who care enough to get involved in their lives and take action on their behalf. People like you. Lots of sermons have been preached about how they brought this man to Jesus, tearing up the roof to make sure he got there so he could be healed, and about all the things that transpired once they lowered him into the house. The story is rich with lessons for us all.

Today, however, I want to focus on a single point from the story. The individuals who carried him that day, and who perhaps changed his clothes and bathed him and fed him all the other days, believed on *that* day the most important thing they could do was to take him to Jesus. I would suggest that is the most important thing you can do for your charge, as well. Go before Jesus on their behalf. If your relationship with them is one that allows it, perhaps you can pray with them, as well as praying for them. Provide opportunity for spiritual conversation, if that is appropriate. At the very least, you can share your experiences of God with them when the moment arises. Maybe your task might be, as has been mine, to help them get ready on Sunday mornings so that they are able to attend worship. Whatever it means in your situation, do not neglect in your caregiving ministry the importance of taking this person to Jesus.

Day 62 Genesis 48:1-11

This is a pretty cool story. After years of separation, Jacob (Israel) was reunited with his beloved son, Joseph, during Jacob's final years. He felt blessed to see his son again and observe the success Joseph had in life, and was surprised to get to meet the grandchildren Joseph had fathered. He embraced and kissed them, and then blessed them. They were privileged to have the opportunity of meeting their grandfather before he went to be with God through the gateway of death.

While I did not think of it this way at the time, I was party to several such incidents in recent years. There was the time before her memory had badly decayed, that my mother and I made a trip to visit with one of her sisters several states away. It was a special time for the two of them, and they had lots of fun talking about old times while looking through photographs. Another time, I drove my 93-year-old father to Chicago where he was able to spend a final time with a brother-in-law who later passed away, and we also enjoyed time with my son as the three of us attended Dad's first ever professional ball game. Another time, Dad and I simply stopped by the home of the widow of a very good friend. I will never forget the smiles and the twinkle in their eyes as they talked about the good times they and their spouses had shared together over the years. And there were several times my parents were invited to travel halfway across the country to spend time with my sister and her family for holidays. For my parents, it always seemed like an insurmountable challenge, but with my encouragement and support, together we all made the necessary arrangements and made sure all the complicating details could be handled. I am sure those times are etched forever into the hearts and minds of my nephews. Those are some of my stories. Are there some you could share as well?

If the one you care for is experiencing the approach of life's end, then this may be the perfect time to make sure there are opportunities for the connections that will never happen again. I suspect Ephraim and Manasseh never forgot their grandfather's pleasure at meeting them that first time, or the feel of his hands upon their heads as he pronounced his prayer of blessing over them. Are you making some of those unforgettable moments happen with the one you love, both for yourself and for others who are special in their sight? It is a great gift to give someone whose days on earth are numbered, and can be a great blessing for those who come.

Day 63 John 20:11-18

One of the hardest things about caregiving is having to make decisions in regard to various life-sustaining medical procedures. A time may come in which the doctors you consult offer various options that can extend the life of your loved one, but may not produce a desirable quality of life. As caregiver, some or part of the responsibility for making that choice may fall to you. How do *you* go about making those decisions?

For some of us, our charge is fully aware and able to make his or her own decisions, or at least help in the decision-making process, and that is a tremendous blessing. Not everyone has that assistance available to them. Another great help is if your loved one has produced a living will, which provides you with insights into how he or she would most likely choose if able to voice the decision. Such a document can provide guidance as you seek to discern what the anticipated desires would have been. (It might also make you consider whether you are making things easier for those who might have to care for you, too!)

Even so, when that moment of decision comes, sometimes people balk at following through on the guidance provided. That can happen because it is so hard to let go, or because the responsibility of the decision just seems too difficult. It might be that there is uncertainty about medical possibilities that might offer alternative hope. There can be lots of reasons for hesitation.

I have had several times in my own experience when treatment options were presented, and I was alone in the moment needing to give emergency guidance. Though I knew the decision I made was in accordance with the desires of my loved one, and suspected that other family members would have concurred, it was still a difficult decision to make. Even after making the decision, it was even more difficult to articulate the choice…because it felt like signing a death warrant. If things did turn in a negative direction, I knew it would have been the words I spoke that determined the doctors' decisions which resulted in physical death.

With all the decisions and emotions in times like these, the words of Jesus to Mary can provide some degree of encouragement and guidance, even though the circumstances are different. Jesus spoke these words to Mary after he had already died and been resurrected. I want to highlight one part of His statement to her: "do not cling to me."

It is one thing to provide care that preserves life for a loved one; it is another to provide that care because I am not willing to let that loved one go. Hard as it may be, there is a time in which you and I have to be willing to let go of the ones we love. Selfishly, certainly we would rather continue spending time with those significant people in our lives, especially if life has been good for them to the end. But life doesn't always provide that option. Yet, it helps to know that when I let go here, my loved one ascends to the Father, Who will never let them go throughout all eternity.

MY PRAYER FOR YOU THIS WEEK

My prayer for you this week is that you will be confident in your right to say, "No," as you set boundaries and the do the things that are necessary for your own physical, emotional, mental and spiritual health. May you be able to release any associated guilt, knowing both that you have done your job well and that, to continue doing it well, you must also tend to your own needs. Amen.

Day 64 Exodus 18:16-23

The people of Israel needed somebody to help them figure out right from wrong, to decide their legal arguments. Moses knew that. And so he tried to meet the need. By himself. After all, who knew better what God wanted than the man who had talked with God personally up on Mount Sinai?!? He had the experience, he had the responsibility; he would simply have to be the one to do it. His father-in-law Jethro told him, in effect, that it was nuts to try to do it all himself. (Kind of makes me wonder if Jethro's daughter hadn't talked to her dad about being worried for Moses's health and sanity!)

Are you trying to do it all yourself? Do you feel that you are the only one who can effectively handle the tasks of caregiving? Have you taken on more than one person can possibly do? Would Jethro suggest that maybe what *you* are trying to do is nuts, too? Would he suggest to you, too, that it is time to call in some reinforcements? Maybe a respite provider or a person with nursing skills would be helpful to include in your caregiving plan. At some point, being responsible may even require us to hand over the responsibility to another team, such as those in a care facility.

One of the critical keys for Moses in leadership was to learn his limits, and to learn how to share responsibility. Those are important things to learn in caregiving, too. Have you figured them out for yourself yet? God does not expect you to be a superhuman able to handle everything. He didn't expect it from Moses, and he doesn't expect it from you. Know your limits, and then enlist help for what is beyond your ability. Jethro wisely counseled Moses that knowing your limits and delegating responsibility are key to being able to endure.

Day 65 Matthew 5:38-42

Have you ever heard the expression, "going the extra mile"? Did you realize it came from this teaching of Jesus? It is in the midst of a passage where Jesus discusses the way we respond to those who treat us poorly, and He teaches us to show the love of God even to our enemies. The passage includes the idea of giving to anyone who seeks to borrow from us and giving an extra article of clothing instead of just one. The core of the teaching is to simply treat people better than they deserve, with actions based upon the love of God, not based on the character of the recipient.

This is actually not a passage that addresses our situation. That is, it isn't talking about how we take care of somebody we love, somebody who is our own responsibility. And yet, if this is how Jesus says we ought to treat those who are enemies and troubling persons, what would He say about how we should treat loved ones? So the concept of this passage does apply to our situation as well. Consider a few thoughts with me.

When you do things for this person in your charge, are you the kind of person who does what you have to, or one who "goes the extra mile" by doing other things beyond the basic necessities? I'm sure there are times when energy and time constraints limit your actions to a minimum. If not, then your situation is far different from mine! But setting those times aside, in general, do you find yourself doing extra, giving a bit more, taking on tasks for this loved one that are over and above? These kinds of actions speak well of your character, but also are a good witness for those who are observing the way you care.

Whenever you can, I encourage you to find ways to do something beyond the bare minimum, even if it means that you have to cut corners on something else. After your work is done and you look back, you will look back with satisfaction, knowing you have done something profound as you shared love God's way. And those who look on will see in your actions a glimpse of the character of God. You won't have these opportunities forever, so make the most of them while you can.

Day 66 Matthew 14:15-16

Sometimes we really want God to do something in the situations around us. We pray and ask Him to intervene, to heal, to deliver or to do all sorts of things. Sometimes, though, we don't recognize what God is doing, while other times, we don't recognize that God is the One doing whatever it is. For example, we may long for God to remove us from a difficult situation while God is instead, using that very situation to strengthen us and to teach us patience or trust. Or we could receive a contact for a job offer that would require us to move to a different location and hesitate, believing that God is using us where we are and would never want us to move, when in fact that very contact may be the way God is calling us to a new ministry in a new location. These are questions we need to be in prayer about regularly if we are going to be people who follow God's guidance.

In the story of the miraculous feeding of over five thousand with the simple loaves and fish, the disciples were keenly aware of the great need. They came to Jesus suggesting that something needed to be done....in their minds, it was time to call it a day. But Jesus chose to meet the need by having *them* do something. They literally became the agents God used to work a mighty miracle, as the food multiplied in their hands. And the little boy who offered his lunch turned out to be the messenger God had sent to provide the tools for the miracle. The disciples were very surprised at how Jesus answered the needs of the moment.

I remember one time when my father had slipped, and lying on the floor he was hesitant to move much in case he had broken something. He didn't call me, because he knew that a chaplain friend of his was coming by soon, so he decided to wait. The chaplain arrived and entered the house when Dad called out to him. What the chaplain thought was going to be a simple visit became instead a mission of mercy when he alerted me and then helped me get Dad to the doctor. Some would call that coincidence. I call it a God thing.

You may have prayed for the needs of the one in your care. Others may have been praying that God would take care of this person. The individual may have offered that very prayer as well! As the caregiver, has it ever occurred to you that *you* are an answer to prayer? Or that you are the hands of God, meeting the needs of a person and thus allowing yourself to be the agent that God uses in answer to prayer? Don't underestimate what God may be doing through your deeds of kindness.

Day 67 Matthew 25:34-40

There is a flip side to yesterday's comments. Not only might you be the very answer to prayer God is using in the situation, your perception of the situation can also be critical in understanding what God is doing.

Have you ever considered carefully the words of Jesus in today's text, in light of the care you are giving to the individual now depending on you? Jesus claimed that when we visit the sick, we actually are visiting him! He considers each caring deed you do as done personally for Himself. You may not realize the divine ministry of what you are doing, but He does. Each wet cloth on the forehead is an act of worship. Each soothing and comforting word is a prayer. Each meal prepared is a precious offering. Jesus receives the deeds you do as if you are doing them personally for him.

If we can visualize Jesus in that wheelchair, lying on that bed or needing help with a walker or the commode, it may not only make us realize how important our help really is, it may also change the manner in which we do our service. Take a few minutes to think about the person you care for, and as you focus on him or her, imagine that this person is Jesus in disguise, waiting to see how you will treat him. And He receives each loving act of service as an offering gift to him. Serve this loved one the same way you would serve Christ were He in the situation, for in truth, it is actually Christ that you serve!

Day 68 James 1:27

What is worship to you? How do you measure whether or not somebody is really a Christian? By how regularly they attend worship? By the church offices they have held, or the classes they have taught? By how well they know the Bible, or by how good a person they are? By whether they prayed a "sinner's prayer" and have been baptized?

Certainly those things are important, and the last ones especially are critical for one's relationship with God. But James challenges our thinking. He tells us that the most pure and truest experience of Christian religion is found in visiting orphaned children and widows in their tough times. Does not the person you are caring for fit into that category? Even if they are not widowed or orphaned, they fall into the realm of being somewhat helpless and at risk and in need of care and protection, which is exactly the point of need for the widows and orphans James mentions. Today, I want to draw and underline and add exclamation points to the things I mentioned yesterday about the sacredness of your tasks. Though it may not always feel like it, the service you are giving now is what, in God's sight, being a Christian is really all about.

Why would that be the case? Because as James made clear throughout his letter, a relationship with God is more than just putting money in an offering plate, singing songs of worship and folding your hands in prayer over supper. True Christianity is a transformational experience with God that translates into actions that reflect the character of God in our lives. It is showing love in tangible ways. It is choosing to control the words that come out of our mouths and changing the attitudes that shape our behavior. It is giving your life, as Jesus Himself did, by doing the things that will make life better for others. So in our passage today, caring for helpless widows and orphans becomes the perfect example of a life dedicated to something and someone beyond oneself.

Never forget the nobility of what you are doing.

Day 69 Ephesians 5:15-17

If there were a contest to select a theme scripture passage for caregivers, I suspect this might at least be a runner up. There are some really pithy challenges here.

Be wise. That is very hard sometimes, isn't it? There are so many choices to make, many of which you must make within the constraints of limited knowledge and limited time.

Don't be foolish. That isn't exactly the same thing, is it? Sometimes, in the press of all the emotions, we worry that we are acting stupidly, or might get carried away by feelings of the moment.

Then we are told to understand what the will of the Lord is. Easier said than done, right? At the core, the will of the Lord can be summed up with the words "love" and "salvation." But sometimes the particulars are hard to discern.

Tomorrow, we will talk about the middle of our passage, the reference to our handling of time and opportunities. But today, I want you to consider the choices you have made and are making. Are you able to see the wisdom in your actions? Remember, just because it may seem foolish to some people, does not mean it is foolish before God, right? And finally, have you made your choices with a commitment to follow God's leading, seeking to be a person who reflects His love? You *really are* in a good place in life, and sometimes you know it. But you also need to realize that truth even when things don't feel so good, and this passage from Ephesians can help you recognize that very thing.

Day 70 Ephesians 5:15-17

Yesterday we briefly covered the phrases surrounding the core of this passage. Today, let's look at that core. Depending on your translation, the phrase says we are to redeem the time, or to make the most of every opportunity. One place this clearly applies is in our contacts with those outside the faith, that we never neglect to cultivate in them a love for and understanding of Christ. But I think the phrase is even richer.

Life is short...even though sometimes days and weeks may feel long. Your task as a caregiver has a definite end, one way or another. Each day gives its own opportunity that may never come again. I remember some days when a loved one felt more able to go do something special, or days when their thinking was more cogent and we could discuss things not always discussable.

As illnesses progress, one is aware there are only a certain number of days left in which to give someone a hug, or for that person to be able to enjoy eating a steak. A time may come when you will think it may be the last opportunity to make that trip to see family members, or to plant a flower bed, or to enjoy the beautiful colors of fall. You may arrange a special celebration for what may be the last birthday, or the last Christmas together. Of course, we don't know the timetables for sure, but there is one thing we do know: we have certain opportunities *now* that are not necessarily guaranteed for *tomorrow*.

How are you doing at redeeming your time, at making the most of the opportunities you have within the context of caregiving? And how well do you take advantage of the rare opportunities you may have to restore your own strength and sanity? To the best of your ability, make the most of each opportunity as it comes. Just don't let yourself get so stressed over all the possible meaningful experiences you could create if you had the time, that you end up creating instead a load of guilt over the fact that you simply can't do them all. Real life is, you can only do what you can do. So do the best you can, with the best wisdom you have, to take advantage of the treasured opportunities you encounter day by day.

MY PRAYER FOR YOU THIS WEEK

My prayer for you this week is that you will sense God near to you as you face the grief of watching one you care for decline, struggle and perhaps suffer memory loss. May you be able to accept and mourn the tough things you face, while treasuring the opportunities you have day by day, and celebrating the memories of days gone by. Amen.

Day 71   John 15:1-5

This is one of the beloved passages of the church. The truth of it is so beautifully illustrated by the simple analogy of a vine bearing fruit. No matter where we live in the world, somewhere, somehow, we have some experience of the tie between a plant's root system, and the fruit that is only produced as long as the connections are intact. Every branch blown off an apple tree by a wind storm is condemned to death and will never bear fruit again. It is cut off from its very lifeline of nourishment.

Our lifeline, of course, is our connection with Christ. If we try to step away from that connection and do things all on our own, we are as hopeless as that apple tree branch. Jesus says it very simply, "Abide in me."

Amid the stresses, strains and demands of caregiving, how are you doing at abiding? Has something caused the connection to suffer fracturing? Do you spend vast amounts of your time at the hospital, nursing home or bedside, and find little or no time for abiding in the presence of God? Has the fruitfulness of your life suffered, because you have neglected your relationship with God as you have gotten caught up in other things? Perhaps today you could make steps to develop that connection afresh, that you may become even more fruitful, living out the life of Christ on a daily basis.

There are often Bibles in the patient rooms and the waiting rooms or chapels of hospitals. A nurse might be able to point you to a place where you could be alone and find a few moments of quiet to pray. Or, perhaps when your charge has fallen asleep and your own eyes become heavy, as you fade into sleep you can do so with a prayer on your lips. Abiding in Christ is what will keep you nourished.

Day 72 John 21:18-22

In life, there are lots of times we do things because we enjoy them and so make time for them in our lives. But then, there are things that we do whether we enjoy them or not, because they simply *have to* be done. In my life, paying bills each month and preparing my tax records fit strongly in the "*have to*" category. In caregiving, the list is almost endless.

Some of us enter the role of caregiver because we choose to do so. Others enter that role because we happen to be in a particular situation when the need arises, and something simply needs *to* be done. However, caregiving is such that, regardless of how you get into it, every day you face tasks you would rather not do, tasks you wish you didn't even have to face, but they are tasks you know *have to* be done.

As the days go by, we may even wonder why things have turned out the way they have. When faced with all the tasks, it is easy to wonder why WE have to do these things... why couldn't a sibling do them, or a nurse, or anybody else...we just don't like doing all the things we *have to* do, and given an option out, we'd let somebody else do them. But there may not be somebody else. And the tasks DO have to be done. So we do them.

Jesus warned Peter that a day would come when he would have to go somewhere he didn't want to go, referring to the path that eventually led to Peter's death. Peter heard the words, then pointed to his fellow disciple, John, and asked (in effect), "Yeah, well, what about HIM? What does HE have to do? Why me?" Jesus replied to Peter with instructions that were, in my opinion, some of the most important words Jesus ever said. Again, in my paraphrase, He told Peter that the plans for John weren't really any of Peter's business, but that Peter was to focus on following Jesus and only on following Jesus. In other words, it's as though He said, "It doesn't matter what anybody else is doing, YOU follow ME!"

When you are facing things that are hard, things you'd rather not be doing, don't allow yourself to get distracted by what other people are or are not doing, or whether or not it is fair that you are having to do the hard thing. Instead, recognize that the hard things you are facing are simply part of following Jesus in this time of your life. Focus on that, and you will be exactly where God wants you to be, doing exactly what God wants you to do. Whether it is easy or hard, whether it is the same as what anybody else is doing or not, your job and mine, just like Peter's, is to follow Jesus. That's all that matters.

Day 73 Exodus 20:17

I don't think I covet other people's things; do you think you ever do? Though it may sometimes appear that things would be easier if I had everything I thought I needed, I'm basically content with the blessings I have received in life. In caregiving, I think there are times that feelings may arise that verge on coveting, or tempt us in that direction, though not in ways usually thought of as coveting.

For example, do you resent that a sibling can just pick up and go whenever they want, while you are tied to the responsibility of caring for your parent? Maybe you are jealous of friends who have the freedom to come and go on the various errands of the day, whereas every errand is a huge undertaking for you, because you have to arrange a substitute or go through a lot of complicated steps to be able to take your charge with you. Maybe your career and finances have been placed on hold, while those around you have continued onward and upward, and you wonder how far behind you have gotten to be. You could probably fill in the blank of some other ways you wish your life were more like somebody else's, whenever you feel trapped in the current situation.

All of these scenarios are like the "grass is greener on the other side of the fence" syndrome. Focusing on the grass over there, verges on coveting something that does not belong to you. God has a specific calling on your life during this time. If you spend your time focusing on the situation of *other* people, instead of on what God is expecting of you just now, you will never appreciate what God is doing in your life. And caregiving is not only about the person you aid, it is also about what God is doing in and for you!

Day 74 Psalm 116:15-19 and Hebrews 2:14-16

Caregiving is very often something we do for someone until that person reaches the end of life's journey here on earth. It is a hard thing to lose someone you care deeply about, as they slip from this life into eternity. And each time we encounter such a loss, it can also remind us of the fact that, one day, it will be our turn to step into eternity to be with God. It is a journey we all must one day make, unless we are privileged to be among those alive at the moment of His return.

God's view of this experience is that it is a precious thing. He came to free us from the fear of death and to conquer what 1 Corinthians 15:26 refers to as the last enemy, and because He conquered death we can know death is not the end. One of the promises of Revelation is that when all things are restored as the new heaven and new earth, there will no longer be any death. But during this interim period, death is the one thing that awaits every human being, regardless of station, ability, intelligence or anything else. Jesus tasted death for us, that we may forever taste life in him.

And so, until that final restoration, the death of His saints is precious to God. I believe each time a dear saint dies, Jesus comes personally to offer a welcome into the heavenly home prepared specially for her or him. It is a moment Jesus would never miss; it is simply too precious. I believe He comes to the side of His beloved at the moment of entry into eternity. And, if your charge is terminal for any reason, you are God's agent on this side in your loved one's precious advance into eternity.

Day 75 John 11:30-36

Did you ever wonder why Jesus wept? After all, He knew that Lazarus would be raised from the dead; He had already told His disciples as much. Yet He wept when Martha, upset over the death of her brother, came to Him. Why?

The scriptures do not tell us exactly why. However, I think that He wept over the awfulness of death and over the pain it causes us when we experience losing a loved one. Especially when He observed up close and personal the awful impact sin has had on what He designed to be a perfect world. How His heart must have ached when He saw Martha and Mary struggling and weeping over the death of their brother. It must have been hard for Jesus to hear their despair and regret that He had not come early enough to have healed their brother. I believe His heart broke as He observed the broken heartedness of His dear friends. I think He still has that compassion today.

In other words, His tears were for people like *you!* People who experience the struggle with sorrow, suffering, loss and death. People who find that days can be too hard or that the task is greater than their endurance. And His tears were for people like the one you care for, whose bodies or minds face the decay of an earthly progression toward death, the destructive force brought into the world by sin.

So perhaps in our caregiving we come closest to the tears of Jesus, as He stopped to weep on His way to Lazarus's tomb. Close because He weeps knowing the sorrow we ourselves carry for the struggles of one we love. And close because our tears mingle with His as we minister in tender mercy to the needs those struggles bring, day by day.

Day 76   John 19:23-27

Is it a parent you are responsible for these days? It feels a little backward, doesn't it? After all, this is an individual who cared for you when you were most helpless in life. But now, perhaps the time has come when that parent is feeling somewhat helpless, and it is *your* help that is needed. I have found it difficult to watch these once vibrant individuals who were pillars of strength in my life, decline and start to see me as *their* pillar instead. But there are times when I think that, really, all I am doing is returning the favor. After all they have done for me, it is the least I can do.

I am struck by the fact that Jesus understands both the responsibility to be an honorable child, and how hard that can be. It is amazing to me that in the most agonizing moments of His life, Jesus called out from the cross to His dear friend John, asking Him to take care of His mother, since He would not be around to do so. As the firstborn son, in that culture it was His responsibility to care for her, but He was dying and His mother was going to age without her firstborn to take care of her. Unable to care for her Himself, He made arrangements to be sure the care was provided. There may come a time when the care needed will exceed your ability, and you may have to consider making arrangements as well. Doing so is *not* abandoning your responsibility; it is caring so much you are realistic about your ability and your desire to be sure the care provided is adequate.

It must have been hard for Jesus, to know that she would not be able to count on Him to take care of her the way she had expected. But He knew what His mission was, and the balance had to be found. You will also have to wrestle with life's balance. As you struggle to do so, know that Jesus understands.

Day 77 Revelation 5:6-8

Isn't prayer an amazing thing? I mean, we take it so for granted, but really, to think that the God of all creation, the God Who scattered galaxies across the vast expanse of the universe, delights in listening to every word you utter in prayer, that is amazing! If you have a child, do you remember the first time you heard that child say, "Mommy," or "Daddy?" If you were like me, it made your heart skip a beat and lifted your spirits. And in those days, you couldn't hear it enough, as those delightful words came from the lips of that little child.

God experiences the same delight when we call out His name. Like listening to a travel story from an excited friend, God rejoices with us as we share with Him the experiences and requests of our lives. As a doting parent rushes to a crying child, so God rushes to meet our needs when we cry out to him.

I especially like this image here in Revelation. It's as if every prayer you have ever offered has been collected by God in special containers. Held there as precious gifts, the day will come when God will open the vessels, allowing the treasured words to float upward once again, producing a sweet aroma like incense. Like the collected love letters written by young lovers to be read over and over again, so are your prayers before God.

Take some time now, to visit with this doting God Who loves you more than any of us can ever fully understand. Add another treasure to the vessel of incense. He longs to hear you share the cares of your heart.

MY PRAYER FOR YOU THIS WEEK

My prayer for you this week is that God will speak through your hands. May your hands be like the hands of Jesus: hands of healing, of comfort, strong hands, hands uplifted in prayer and broken in sacrifice...hands God uses. And each time you notice your hands this week, may they remind you of the Master, whose hands minister to you in those ways as you rest safe within his loving embrace. Amen.

Day 78 Hebrews 4:8-11

There are a couple of insights useful for caregivers to be found in today's passage. The first is the highlighting here of the Sabbath, a Hebrew word that actually means, "rest." When you put that into the context of the Ten Commandments with the instruction to remember the Sabbath day to keep it holy, the implication is that we are to keep a day not only for worship, but also as a day of rest *as a holy priority*. Are you doing that, these days? Are you maintaining a faithful involvement in worship with a community of believers? Do you actually spend that day in both worship and rest? They both need to be priorities.

In the teaching of Hebrews, Sabbath rest is found through Christ, because in Him we rest from working for approval from God. Our standing and approval with God are received, instead, as a grace gift. As a result, we can rest in the completed work of our salvation. That is a key point of the book of Hebrews.

Today, I want us to consider the purpose of rest. It is to regain strength and be refreshed, isn't it? That is, rest helps us find new energy and life?   To allow all the wounds and wear and tear of the day to be healed and restored? If these are the purposes of rest, doesn't it seem fitting to you to think of Jesus as providing our rest? Doesn't God promise us strength, renewal, healing?

My point is simply this: while you may not have a lot of time for physical rest and vacations during the time of caregiving, you can recognize that your real rest is found in Christ. Therefore, never neglect to turn to Him regularly as your source of strength and revitalization, for Jesus *Himself* is the source of our Sabbath rest.

Day 79   Psalm 13:1-6

It sounds very hard-hearted to say--and if you acknowledge the feelings to yourself, you can feel very guilty--but after days, months or years of caregiving, there are days you wonder how long it is going to last. Depending on your particular situation, there may or may not be a "light at the end of the tunnel." I have known caregivers caring for children with severe physical or mental handicaps that are so great, the individual is aware it has become their lifelong commitment. I have known caregivers who have stepped in for the final few months of an elderly or terminally ill person's life. And then there are those who care for parents, spouses or others, knowing that the end will come, but not sure whether it will take weeks, months, or years.

It is okay that your heart cries, "How long, O Lord," with the Psalmist. Because caregiving can be very long. And, even if it isn't very long, it can feel very long. A prayer like this is an honest way to cry out to God for the strength to endure. No matter how long it takes. How honest are your prayers with God, these days? Perhaps today might be a good time to cry out with the honest questions you have about the struggles you face. God will grant His strength as you need it, day by day, and sometimes moment by moment. How long, O Lord? The Lord's answer may well be, "However long it takes."

Day 80 Psalm 19:7-10

I have a habit of doing daily Bible reading, including the reading of daily devotionals such as this one. I have done so for many years, using a variety of aids and plans. I have a couple of booklets I am using these days, and I am currently behind. Like a couple of weeks behind. For a variety of reasons, the last few weeks have just been very difficult, leaving little time to concentrate on those items, and I feel very ragged. And truthfully, I don't know which leaves me more ragged, all the load of the tasks I do, or missing some of those daily devotions. Those morning times may accomplish more than I even realize! At least, that was the experience described by David in today's passage.

I will catch up on them. This has happened before, and I always make myself catch back up...sometimes reading four or five days' worth at a time. I do this because I don't want to miss out on what might be in the readings. And also because that time with the Lord is important for me, and I figure I really do need to make up for the time lost if I want to keep the relationship strong. It isn't enough to just be praying; the time in the scriptures is also critical, because it actually brings renewal for me. Relationship with God means not only time for me to speak with God, but also time for God to speak to me in His Word.

When life is hurried and harried, when you don't think you have time to spend in the scriptures or in prayer and you feel you have been worn ragged, make time. *Force yourself* to make time, some kind of time. Maybe it will only be thirty seconds when you first get into your car. Maybe it will be reading one or two verses with tired eyes at night. Or maybe you can set aside one morning a week to rise early, go out to some quiet park or lake and spend a few hours alone with God and the scriptures. However you do it, **make it happen!** It never "just happens," or is "convenient," or occurs automatically. You literally have to choose to make it happen. It is important to do, for *that* is one of the most primary means God uses to restore the tired and troubled soul.

Day 81 Isaiah 42:1-4

God's care for our lives is so tender, so gentle, so loving. The bruised reed He won't break, the flickering wick He won't extinguish. Though bruised and unusable, though the oil is gone and the light is about to disappear, God never gives up in His care for us.

This pattern of tender care is reflected in your life with every washcloth you use, every batch of laundry you wash, every time you load a wheelchair or walker into the car or van, every time you do anything to make the life of the person in your care just a little bit easier. The work you do, the attitude it takes, is, in fact, the very work of God and the perfect reflection of His character. YOU are participating in the tender, loving care God has for each and every one of His created beings.

At the same time, I remind you that this is how God cares for *you*, too. When you can barely carry on, God will carry you. When your strength begins to wane, His strength will come to renew. When you cannot see the way before you, God's light will illuminate the path. When you feel like you are at the end of your rope, God will extend His hand for you to grasp instead. Receive, and then pass on His loving care. It is a wonderful God we have, indeed.

Day 82 Ephesians 4:26

This seems kind of an odd verse to include in a devotional for caregivers, doesn't it? After all, aren't caregivers the folks who are always looking out for somebody else, going the extra mile and doing lots of tasks (some not so pleasant) for somebody else? Well, yes they are, but...

I know that there were times as I was carrying out the various responsibilities I have had, that I would get a bit too stressed, a bit too frazzled, and end up being a *lot* too irritable! And I'm not particularly proud to admit that sometimes that irritability came out in the form of short temperedness with the individuals I cared for, as I was dealing with their various requests and needs. I'd snap at them, or get unnecessarily upset and stressed. I'm not much of a yeller or door slammer, but I didn't need to do those things for them to be able to recognize that I was upset.

Today's passage isn't telling us to be angry like that, I don't think. I think Paul is trying to teach us appropriate ways to deal with anger, and there is, indeed, a useful place for anger with such things as injustice. My anger certainly didn't fit the bill, though! On the other hand, the passage also tells us that in dealing with anger, we need to deal with it on a daily basis, rather than let it fester.

If you blow your stack, and know you were out of line, don't let it carry over. The truth is, with the stresses of caregiving, there will likely be days it is all too easy to get irritable. Sometimes it comes out on your charge, sometimes on your family, or you may even unwittingly

take it out on the clerk at the grocery store! Before the
sun sets, make your apologies directly to the person
involved, take it to God in prayer, and then *let it go!* Don't
expect yourself to be perfect. Instead, expect yourself to
be a person who handles your imperfections responsibly...
especially when anger gets the best of you.

Day 83 1 Thessalonians 4:13-14

I like this passage a lot. It is often used at funerals, and
sometimes misused at them, too. At some point in time
there is a good chance that you, as a caregiver, are going to
experience grief at the loss of the one for whom you are
caring. As we have mentioned elsewhere, discussing
spiritual matters with your charge is an important and good
thing to do...for both of you. For your charge, having
spiritual matters clarified and settled means one can face
the inevitable end of life with faith and hope. For you,
when your loved one is gone, you will have the assurance of
that loved one's eternal destiny. And that changes
everything: from how you will have discussed the illnesses
that have brought the decline, to the hope you both will
have of reuniting at Jesus' feet.

In 1 Thessalonians, Paul acknowledged that grief is part
of life, the natural response to the loss of a loved one
through death. But Paul advised us that believers grieve
differently than those who do not know Christ. Because we
know that Jesus rose from the grave, we know that the
death of our earthly bodies is not the end of the story.
Unlike those who speculate that life goes on somehow, we
know by faith that it does, because we know personally
Someone Who lived beyond the grave. And when we also
know that someone we care for has committed his or her
life to Christ, we know that heaven is what awaits that
person after they leave this earthly life. As a result, our
grief is for the separation and loss *we* experience, not for
the one who has died and now dwells in glory. As Paul

suggested, let this knowledge bring comfort to you and yours in Christ. We do not grieve without hope.

Day 84 Proverbs 17:17

Often, when someone is a caregiver, there is an awareness that there is an entire family looking over your shoulder, maybe even second guessing many of the decisions. Many of us have been blessed with families who are supportive of what you are doing, resulting in a wonderful team approach that can be very helpful in times of uncertainty or crisis. Even if you have been blessed with a supportive family, there may well be times when you face decisions that must be made by you. Sometimes they must be made on the spur of the moment, and whether you have time to consult with other family members or not, the final decision rests upon you as you make choices and express your wishes to the doctors, accountants, or other individuals involved with the care of your loved one.

It is within the nature of family life that different individuals are going to perceive things differently. You can garner opinions, do your research, consult with experts and make the best possible choice you know how to make, but there is always the chance somebody is going to disagree. Especially if things don't turn out the way you anticipated. While others may get caught up in debates, reliving the past and Monday morning quarterbacking, *you* give yourself permission to know that sorting all those things out is NOT what you have been called to do. You have been called to do the best you can in looking out for the best interests of the one you care for, and if you have done that, then you can have a clear conscience before God in the choices. That, my friend, is worth all the wealth in the world!

MY PRAYER FOR YOU THIS WEEK

My prayer for you today is for your renewal. May your weariness be transformed to strength, your discouragement to hope and your sense of struggle into an awareness of great accomplishment. And as these things happen, may you be renewed and ready to face one more day, one more task, one more challenge. Amen.

Day 85 Hebrews 1:13-14; 2:5-7

Hollywood has a pretty confused theology, with lots of feel good notions of white light and a heaven, but no hell... sometimes with a belief that people come back over and over again through reincarnation. The definition of good people and the understanding of how one makes it to heaven are very strange in much of Hollywood, apparently. But perhaps the strangest of all is their notion of the origin of angels. In Hollywood...and then, as a sad result, in the minds of too many Christians...angels are what people become after they die. But that is not at all biblical.

This passage in Hebrews makes clear that angels are not humans. In fact, they are a different class of created spiritual beings sent by God to minister to the needs of believers, the saints. Paul even says in 1 Corinthians 6:3 that we are going to be their judges! Having said that, though, I want to mention that the Greek "angel" (which is basically, "angel"--"angellos") has the very simple meaning of "messenger." Sometimes in the scripture it is used to refer to the heavenly spiritual beings, but sometimes it is used to refer to human messengers as well. The same is true of the Hebrew word; sometimes it is translated as a human messenger, sometimes it refers to heavenly messengers and is translated as angel.

Okay, so I said all that simply so that I could clearly say the following: in many ways, *you* are acting the part of an angel for somebody. There are even caregiving businesses that adopt use the word "angel" in the business name. You are *not* an angel like the angelic beings of heaven, and you will never be that. *However*, just as angels are ministering spirits, so you are ministering to the person in your care and, in a very tangible way, bringing the message of God's love and tender mercies into the life of a person in need. We all need the ministry of angels, messengers of God, to keep us going in life--sometimes heavenly ones, sometimes earthly ones. Right now, *you* are that messenger for someone special!

Day 86 2 Kings 6:15-17

Yesterday we talked about the nature of angels a bit, and your role as a human messenger (angel) on behalf of God. There truly is something special about participating with God in the work He is doing in our world, and in the life of someone we care about. This concept of participating with God is very important, and I want to expand upon it.

Today's reading contains this wonderful story about Elisha and his attending servant, Gehazi. They were in a dangerous place, surrounded by enemy forces seeking to capture the city, then kill or enslave the inhabitants. Gehazi was scared; Elisha was confident. Why the difference? Because Elisha could see (or at least knew) what Gehazi did not. That is, not until Elisha prayed and God opened Gehazi's eyes. All around the city were God's warrior angels, heavenly beings protecting and encompassing the people of God. Gehazi was astounded by the sight, transformed from his fear into a state of wonder by what he saw. Wouldn't it be something if we, like Gehazi, had the opportunity to actually see with our physical eyes God's warrior angels standing for *us* in our world?

Might I suggest an image for your consideration today? As you are being used by God in this way during this time, I suspect that, if you could but see as Gehazi saw, you would see that every time you walk into the room where your special charge awaits you, there are angelic beings at your side, and at that person's side as well. Each time that person nearly slips, there is an angel's hand steadying your grip, supporting that loved one. When you wipe a brow, wash a face, change a bandage, whatever you do, the hands of angels are upon yours, adding the special blessing and comfort of God to all that you do.

Perhaps if you watch very closely, you might catch a glimpse of one of those messengers beside you. But even if you don't, you can have the confidence Elisha had, that God has already arranged all the help you need for every task and challenge that faces you. That's true for today, and for every day of your life.

Day 87 Genesis 27:15-23

Failing eyesight with multiple trips to get glasses continuously adjusted. Hearing loss that results in obtaining hearing aids that may or may not work very well. Bones that are fragile, and can break with a simple bump. Balance that begins to be compromised. Old age is a wonderful thing, huh? Actually, there *are* some great things about old age. These are just some of the challenges that come with it.

In this story, the reason Isaac was supposedly unable to recognize that it was Jacob and not Esau he was blessing was that his eyesight was failing in his old age. However, some commentators suspect—and I think rightly so—that Isaac had to have known it was Jacob, and that this ruse was Rebekah's way of "saving face" for Isaac as he did a hard thing. That is, Rebekah was helping Isaac have the courage to bless God's chosen son instead of the one Isaac himself preferred, and therefore her intent would have been to provide an easier way for him to be obedient to God's desires.

Anyway, if the person you care for is an aging parent or loved one, the toll of old age on the body can make things very difficult. Repeating statements multiple times because the individual didn't hear you can be frustrating, at best. But then, having to ask to be told again must be frustrating as well, wouldn't you suppose?

Are there hard things that need to be done that you can help make happen in such a way that they provide a blessing? There may be some face-saving ways you need to employ to help a loved one do some difficult things. Things like helping to adjust clothing in a discreet way, or helping an Alzheimer's patient know the words needed for a phrase that they just can't quite put together. It may be difficult for you to drop everything to run over for what seems like a trivial matter to you...but what a blessing to them that you are there! Remember, at this time of a loved one's life, dignity is a precious gift to give.

Day 88 Psalm 62:6-8

Have you seen, when watching war movies, or maybe old westerns, a scene where someone is caught out in the open during some kind of gunfight or battle? The individual would often seek out a rock to hide behind and peer over to return fire, while bullets bounced off the rock that protected him. In other situations, you might see somebody clinging to a rock, trying to hang on as the winds and waves try to sweep them away. I have seen this sort of thing in survival photos of tsunami disasters. Haven't you?

A rock as a refuge is a powerful image when you feel as though the tempests of life are raging out of control. God promises to be *your* rock, to be *your* refuge, to shelter *you* and protect *you* and give *you* the stability that can be found nowhere else.

Okay, so all of that sounds pretty good, but the question is, how do you make it happen? At this time, I live fairly close to Joplin, Missouri. Not so long ago, Joplin was hit by a major tornado that devastated about a third of the city. I actually remember that day, because the tornadic clouds were swirling and forming over us on their way east. I was outside, watching the weather (I love storm clouds!) and listening for warning sirens. The largest hailstones I have ever seen fell sprinkled over my yard, and I watched as the hail first blew down from the south, then from the north, and finally at a strong slant from the east. I knew then that this was an unusual storm indeed! After the devastation in Joplin, stories emerged of individuals who had survived by taking shelter one way or another, just as I would have had the sirens sounded where I lived. I remember especially the story of some individuals who had been in a convenience store, and survived by all taking refuge in the large cooler. When they emerged, the flimsy sheet metal building was gone, but the cooler had endured the storm and kept them safe. That is finding refuge in a storm! I was in Joplin myself within a day or two, and passed by the area where that convenience store stood. It is amazing anybody survived at that location. But then, that is the power of a good refuge and shelter!

So back to the question, how do you actually make God your refuge? Let me use that Joplin incident to illustrate some suggestions. First, the shelter did no good for any who did not choose to enter. If God is going to be your shelter, you need to go to Him and seek the strength and protection that He offers by asking Him for it. Next, for the shelter to work, the customers had to obey the instructions of the storekeeper, who knew how the latches operated and where the cooler was located. God's Word contains plenty of instructions about how we are to live our lives. We cannot ignore them and expect to be safely sheltered. Another lesson is that the time to enter the shelter is before the storm turns nasty. Had the people waited until the tornado hit the building to run for the shelter, the story would have had a far different ending. Are you quick to turn to God for help in your times of struggle, or is He merely that last resort? Finally, you have to ride out the storm, safely sheltered in your refuge. Those individuals would have been foolish to step out of the cooler while glass and other debris were swirling outside the door. By waiting within, the cooler bore the brunt of the storm, rather than the people themselves.

Making God your refuge is not something accomplished in a single day. You must continue to draw near to Him and seek His aid day by day, moment by moment, until the time comes that you are on the other side of the storm. You have to allow Him to handle the raging tempest when you cannot, instead of trying to step out of His shelter to fix everything yourself. Sometimes in life we have to simply wait it out, and trust that God is doing something even if we cannot see it or change it ourselves.

With all the uncertainties that swirl around you as you are involved in caring for another human being in difficult circumstances, having a rock to cling to may be the only thing that will get you through some days. But that strong shelter and refuge that is God can keep you safe through all of life's storms, if you but enter in. Hold on tight, and realize as you hang on, that God also holds on to *you*.

Day 89   Isaiah 30:1-5, 15-18

In what is your trust placed these days? I mean, really, what *are* you trusting in? Is it in your ability to figure things out, as you make the various plans and decisions bound up with caring for a loved one? Is it the insurance company who helps with the bills? Is it your own strength to get you through each day? Is it that you expect the day will come when you will be released from the burdens of care and be able to move in a new direction? Or that you look to respite care and other people to come in, so that you can get the rest and release you need, even if only temporarily?

When today's scripture was originally written or proclaimed, the people of Israel had already received multiple revelations from God and had the scriptures available, along with prophets and priests who could teach them God's desires for their lives. In spite of those things, their trust was elsewhere. They were looking for people, specifically the people of Egypt, to be their source of deliverance, their protection, and to help secure their future. That actually sounds to me a lot like our modern world's political alliances in which God is frequently left out of the equation, or in the ways that so many people these days only turn to God in the midst of disaster.

God makes clear in this passage that this limited trust is foolish, and that real rest and security can only be found by returning to and trusting in God. The image of verse 18 is very powerful, where Isaiah explicitly says that God is more ready to help you and me than we are ready to come to Him for that help! Let me repeat that: *God is more ready to help you and me than we are ready to come to Him for that help!* His mercy is waiting for your call. His plans will always succeed. His rest endures forever. If you have time, I encourage you to reread this passage slowly, asking yourself along the way, "Where do *I* really put my trust?"

Day 90   Philippians 4:19

God promises to meet our needs. Unfortunately, we often are not able to make the distinction between needs and wants, or between what *we* think are needs and what God knows to be actual needs in our lives.

For instance, at this point of my life, I live in a rather large house, with several bedrooms, that we are in the process of remodeling. However, helpful as that space is when we have company, or to make available to those who would have need of such space, it is not a real need that we have such space. We *need* shelter. But anyone with a sense of what housing is like around the world or among those living in poverty, realizes that such a house is far beyond the basic need of shelter. We could get by with much less, and know it. It is the temporary project we have undertaken while helping care for my parents.

For many of us, there are plenty of areas in our lives where we think we know what our needs are, but in actuality, the real need might be less or different than what we have come to expect. With all this in mind, it may be useful for you to consider what it is you need right now in your life, as you serve in the role of caregiver. What is it you need from God in this time?

If you are like me, there are plenty of things you could place on a list of wants that you believe would make life easier. But God's promise is to make sure our *needs* are met, not everything we might want. Trust Him to do so, knowing that every real and vital need will find the provision of God. Seek not only to have your needs met, but to understand what it is *God* needs you to have in order to accomplish what God desires in your life.

Day 91 Matthew 11:28-30

Have you ever had to pick up and carry something heavy? I did it just the other day with a friend as we moved an oversized old style television to another home. It was something I was not willing, or able, to do on my own.

It may well be that with all the things you are trying to manage and a schedule overflowing with all the tasks of caregiving, *you* aren't able to do them all effectively by yourself, either. Oh, you can probably do them, but to do them all really well, you need someone willing to carry the other end of your load.

The yoke of old was the binding device that tied two beasts of burden together in such a way that neither of them had to pull the load all by themselves. Jesus has already placed himself into His half of the yoke He offers, and He waits for you to take up His yoke loaded only with the burdens appointed by Him. He offers to share the load with you as you join with Him in prayer and obedience. In fact, the indication is that when you take His yoke upon you, the burden He appoints is itself lighter than all the cares we pile upon ourselves. And I would point out that if you are already serving Jesus in this ministry of caregiving, then you are already joined with Him if you will but realize it and take advantage of the assistance He offers. In that case, your job is to learn to not try to carry your burdens all by yourself; your job is to share the load and partner with One who is much, much stronger than you.

So, how about the yoke of *your* burdens? Are you pulling alone, or have you learned the secret of laying your own yoke down so that you can take up the yoke of Christ, allowing Him to share the load? That is, have you learned through practice the importance of taking your concerns to Christ, of waiting for Him to act in His timing, of believing

His promise that He will give us rest? And, having taken your concerns to Christ, have you learned to not pick them up again, but to bring them back to His throne over and over if necessary, rather than continue to carry burdens you have given to Him? Have you learned to do the things you know to do, to leave with Him the things that are not yours to do, and how to discern which are which? Have you learned the importance of making time with God a priority? This may be a good day to start releasing burdens you have gathered for yourself. After all, the biggest secret to sharing the yoke with Christ is to practice. And the result, according to Jesus, will be rest for your soul.

MY PRAYER FOR YOU THIS WEEK

My prayer for you today is that you will find ways to know how much you are appreciated for all you do. That you will see a grateful look in the eye of your loved one, or be reminded that others are not worried about the person because they know you are there. Most important of all, may you be reminded that God notices and appreciates even a cup of cold water that is given in his name. Amen.

Day 92 1 Kings 19:9-19

"What are you doing here?" God repeated the question to Elijah. Elijah was there because he was worried, depressed, discouraged, overwhelmed and just plain weary! God's question and then His commission confronted Elijah with Elijah's own sense of discouragement, and then reminds him the work is not over. Most of all, God reminded him that though he had lost touch and felt very alone, he was not. God had other followers all around Elijah, which means there were people Elijah *could* turn to for needed support and encouragement.

So do you ever get worried? Depressed? Discouraged? Overwhelmed? Weary? Are there days God would need to ask you, "What are you doing here?" Have you gotten so isolated you have forgotten you are not alone? God is there, and there are other believers you could call on if you chose to do so. Have you forgotten that you are where you are because of God's calling, or that the task is not yet done, and that when God gives the call, He also gives the strength to endure? Elijah needed to be reminded of these things, and sometimes, so do we.

The end of the task may come in different ways for different people. For some, it will continue until the death of the loved one. For others, it may be more like Elijah's experience of handing the work on to the next person. We are part of a great work, a work God is doing through each one of us individually, as well as all of us together. When we feel drained, lonely and discouraged, it does not mean God can no longer use us, nor that there are not wonderful works of God ahead yet to be discovered. But it does mean it may be time to gain some perspective, to seek out the encouragement and support we need, as well as time to reexamine the choices and priorities of our lives. Then we will be ready to step out into the next phase of ministry with God as our guide.

Day 93   John 11:25-27

I have said it before, and will say it again: it is tough to watch the decline of someone you love. Each moment is a kind of treasure, even though it doesn't always feel that way. And sometimes, looking back, you feel bad that it didn't feel that way at the time! If your caregiving situation is one in which you are having to watch someone you care for gradually decline, it can be a tremendous encouragement if you know how their story will continue beyond the grave.

Jesus made plain that there is life beyond this life for those who trust and follow him. In so doing, He promised that death is not final, and that any who are His will never truly die. Ever. Eternity is the key. This is knowledge you may need to share with your loved one, if they don't know Him already.

When I see headlines telling me of the discovery of ancient fossils or describing big bangs millions of years ago, my life expectancy of less than a century seems very brief. Imagine how brief it would seem if I could even fathom the concept of eternity, and then use that perspective to compare this earthly life to the eternal one!

You are truly blessed if, in your gradual letting go, you also know that what you are observing is NOT the end of the story for this special person, but the verge of something wonderful far beyond imagination. "Yet shall he or she live," is the way Jesus expressed it to us. It is the essence of hope.

Day 94 Nehemiah 6:1-3

Nehemiah was on a mission: he was out to rebuild the city of Jerusalem, to help reestablish the capital and worship center of the Jewish nation, after it had lain in rubble for years. As often happens with individuals on a mission, he met opposition and criticism when people like Sanballat and Tobiah tried to shut him down. They fed him false rumors, hoping to lure him away from his work. He refused to lose his focus, declaring that he was involved in a great work, and didn't have time to be bothered with stupid rumors.

As a caregiver, your life is probably very focused right now, too. Your schedule may be pretty well mapped out for you day by day, hour by hour. There are things that might distract you from that focus, or individuals who might oppose your choices for one reason or another. On the other hand, things may be going pretty well for you---I don't really know. But I DO know this: just as the work Nehemiah was doing was a great work, so the work you are doing is a great work in the sight of God. Never forget that.

You are doing one of the most significant things a person can do here on earth...even though it will probably never lead you to fame, fortune or being honored in our society. Nevertheless, it *is* a great work, and in the midst of the day to day drudgery...that is a good thing to remember. Strive to maintain a sense of the big picture, just as Nehemiah did. In the long run, you may end up deciding it was the most important thing you ever did in your life!

Day 95 Jonah 2:1-10

I really like this prayer passage. The imagery is so strong, the reality of the struggle so intense and the encouragement of his faith so timely that the passage just really speaks to me in my own times of struggle, especially if my struggle borders on despair.

Not everybody experiences a lot of mood shifts in life. Some people seem to be pretty happy most of the time; others seem to be pretty blue most of the time. And some folks, well it just depends on the day and time you ask. For those of us who have times that we intensely experience discouragement or despair, this little prayer has much to say.

The overwhelming stresses of caregiving can feel much like what Jonah must have felt when the waves swirled over him and seaweed pulled him downward, as described in today's passage. Hopefully, though, the feelings aren't the result of somebody throwing you overboard! (Although...there are times it can sure feel as if you've been thrown overboard, aren't there?) The image of distress as floodwaters surround you and entangling seaweed pulls you downward can be all too real. I believe it is even harder when the seaweed is an invisible downward spiral within, which cannot clearly be seen by others.

If you have days (or weeks!) that feel like this, remember the prayer of Jonah. In the midst of it, it was God to Whom he cried out for help. And, as a friend of mine pointed out, Jonah called out to God in this time even though he didn't deserve God's help. Still, God helped him anyway. Remember that God is also there for you, *even if you don't think you deserve His attention, and even when you cannot readily sense His presence*. Find something for which to be thankful, and offer God the sacrifice of praise and obedience. Then simply hang on for dear life, knowing that you are looking in the right place. Jonah set the example as he believed and admitted forthrightly in his prayer that salvation comes from the Lord. Oh, and by the way, I hope your deliverance comes in a more pleasant way than being vomited out of a fish!

Day 96 Matthew 10:29-31

God knows. That's a pretty broad statement, isn't it? But it is true in the broadest sense you can interpret...and even beyond *that*! God knows every sparrow that falls to the ground...and based on the noise in the trees around my house, that's a lot of birds for Him to be keeping an eye on! God knows every hair on your head. He knows everything there is to know about your situation, your efforts, your hopes, your disappointments, your fears, your faith, your struggles, your salvation, YOU!   God knows.

In times when you feel at the end of your rope, as though you just can't keep going, God knows how you feel. When it seems that nobody understands the stress you are

115

under and how frazzled you feel, God knows. When it seems you are misunderstood, and your actions are scrutinized and your motivation questioned, God knows. If you feel like a failure because you lost your temper, or that you are so unworthy and unlovable that God could never forgive or love you, God knows. When you are faced with hard choices, and aren't sure what you should do, God knows. Even in the moments when you doubt God's love or purpose, when you are angry at God for the situation you are in, or when it seems your faith has withered and died away, God knows. God knows everything you see, think, feel and experience. And everything He does in your life is perfectly adjusted according to that knowledge.

He watches over everything you face in life. He sees your heart and understands how you feel within. He knows when you falter and fall, as well as when you arise and conquer. Gods knows more about you than you do. God knows more about your future than you can imagine. God knows everything that you need. Today, tomorrow...every day of your life. And the point Jesus makes in this passage is that, in knowing, God also provides for every need.

Day 97   Matthew 25:14-21

Have you ever thought about what it would sound like to have Jesus look you square in the eyes, and say to *you*, "Well done, good and faithful servant?" Even the invitation to the Master's joy pales in comparison to the thought of hearing Jesus say those words, don't you think?

The tasks we do are a service to God. God notices on a daily basis each word of encouragement, each gesture, each effort. We will struggle, we will make mistakes, and we will not always accomplish as much as we may desire. But we can be faithful and we can realize that in all that we do, we are actually serving God. It is important to remember for Whom we are doing our work. Sure, we may have begun our caregiving for a loved one because of our love for this person or their need for our help, but ultimately, it is for God, because it is His calling to this work that matters most. And caregiving for another human being is definitely His kind of work!

You know, this passage might actually be worth reading on a daily basis, just as a reminder. What if at the end of each day, when you are weary and worn and asking yourself how much longer it will last, or if it could get any harder, you opened your Bible and read this phrase as if Jesus was saying it to you right then: "Well done, good and faithful servant." It might just make the load a little bit lighter, don't you think?

Day 98   Isaiah 26:3-4

"Perfect peace." That is a pretty profound concept, I'd say, wouldn't you? Absolute, unmarred, unblemished, nothing-better-even-possible kind of peace! Not of your own making, but provided to you by the God Who keeps you in that perfect peace. Sounds almost too good to be true, doesn't it?

Is it hard for you to keep your mind "stayed on him"? It is for me. Life is full of distractions. Problems scream out for me to solve them myself. Many a time I have sat down to read my morning devotions or to spend some time in quiet reflection, only to be interrupted by a phone call beckoning me to come help with one activity or another. Tasks mount up beyond my ability to keep up. And if I am not there for the one in my care, then nobody else is going to be and needs will go unmet. Too often, as all of this happens, there just doesn't seem to be enough time. How, in the midst of all that chaos, can I possibly keep my mind stayed on him?

Honestly, I don't really know how. Because I have to keep going back to it, trying over and again to get back on track in my thinking. But it seems to me that learning to keep my mind on Christ is simply part of an ongoing and developing relationship with Christ, something that may take us a lifetime to learn. By choosing time and to reopen the pages of scripture to absorb the words recorded there for me. And by finding ways to step out of the moment long enough to have a few short minutes of prayer time with God or knowing where the secret places of refuge are where I can be alone with the Lord when the need arises. It can also mean pausing in the midst of the hubbub to consider the possibilities of what God might be seeking to accomplish in me or my world at the moment. And perhaps most of all, it means learning to make prayer the first response in every situation.

I frequently need to be reminded and understand that it is the practice of these disciplines that God uses to provide the power, strength and peace needed to handle the rest of life. Our lifeline with Christ is vital, not optional. That lifeline is the core, not one of the add-ons of life. Once again, I encourage you to put this book down, and focus for a time solely upon God, allowing Him to fill you with just a bit more of His perfect peace.

MY PRAYER FOR YOU THIS WEEK

My prayer for you this week is that as you minister to the one in your care, you will be sowing seeds that will bear good fruit when the time comes for that loved one to depart this earth and for you to say goodbye. As you live and prepare, may your actions prepare you to be able to look back with the satisfaction that comes from a job well done and opportunities wisely used, your heart and mind filled with memories that will be cherished for a lifetime. Amen.

Day 99 Hebrews 6:10 and Luke 17:10

As a caregiver, you perform many tasks that most people have no idea even need to be done. And yet every day, you do them, because doing them is part of being a caregiver. And you do them whether anybody notices or appreciates them or not. I have been very fortunate in that, more than once while caring for my father, he has said himself that though others may not know or appreciate everything I do, *he* knows and *he* appreciates it. You may not have that luxury in the case of your loved one as they may not fully realize the situation or think to express their gratitude. But there is One Who notices, One Who appreciates, and that is God.

This verse in Hebrews reminds us that God is not unjust nor does He ignore all the things you do in service for Him and for others. God knows, and God appreciates, and God will reward. Of course, that isn't the whole basis of why we do what we do...but it is nice to know. God values your work.

At the same time, it is important that we do our tasks with a proper attitude. We do them to please God, as we minister to our loved ones. But it is not something to boast about. That is why I included this verse from Luke, too. I really like the teaching it contains. Yes, you may be working non-stop and nobody appreciates or notices. Yes, you may be doing so many things everybody is totally unaware of, that those things absorb all your time and energy. But you cannot let resentment take hold, or a sense of feeling superior over, say, other family members who do less, or other individuals who handle the same challenge in other ways.

Jesus urges us, in these moments, to simply take the attitude that we are just servants, doing the things God has asked of us. Nothing more, nothing less. And then we trust that He will appropriately reward us in His own time and way.

Day 100 John 21:1-3

It was quite a struggle for the disciples who had followed Jesus for years and believed He would bring a great deliverance, when suddenly He was viciously executed instead. Even though afterward they had seen Him resurrected, they just didn't quite know what to make of it all. Stunned, devastated, overwhelmed...words are hard to find that can adequately describe what they must have felt.

I have always been struck by the conversation in today's passage. After it was all said and done, they had decisions to make. Peter announced that he decided he may as well go back to fishing. I believe that is a very profound statement, revealing the struggle they all were experiencing. Now that they had reached the end of those years of roaming the countryside following Jesus, the time had come to move on in life...if only they could figure out what moving on meant.

There will come a day (perhaps it already has), in which your task of caregiving will come to completion. You will probably experience a multitude of emotions, just as I have along the way. There can be relief that it is over, and guilt that you didn't do more. There can be the satisfaction of knowing you really did make a difference, and tears at the loss of a loved one. But at some point, your life will alter just as the disciples' lives did, and you will have to ask yourself, "What now? Where do I go from here?"

Vast amounts of energy and time that were consumed in your caregiving tasks will suddenly not be required any more. Much of that energy may have already been drained, leaving you weak and depressed. And then you will have to choose what to do with your life, once the caregiving chapter is over.

The disciples didn't understand what they should do at first; it was only later that Jesus made clear their new purpose in life. And even then, their steps forward needed changes and adjustment along the way. It may take some time for you, as well. There may be tears, travel and even a lot of reorganization in your process of restructuring to move on in life. But know this: in His own time and His own way, Jesus will show you where to go and what to do next. In the meantime, go fishing. Or do whatever it is that can keep you moving forward as you await guidance for the next chapter of your life.

EPILOGUE

Well friend, you have reached the end of this collection of devotionals. Odds are, though, you have not reached the end of your caregiving journey. Hopefully, these writings have helped share the load for a portion of that journey and let you know that you are not alone. Others have been in situations similar to yours and, more importantly, God is walking this path with you to carry you through whenever you are not able to manage on your own.

I want to affirm for you one last time that what you are doing is one of the most important things a person can do here on earth. It is a very costly gift to give, but it is a precious gift with great reward. It has been one of the best things I have ever done in my life, and I trust that it will be for you, as well. God bless you through this ministry, and God bless your loved one through you.

Richard

APPENDIX ONE: PROMISES OF GOD & ENCOURAGING SCRIPTURES LIST

The following scriptures are a collection of a few beloved scriptures and promises that I found to be helpful and encouraging in the ministry of caregiving. They may be helpful not only for you, but also for the one in your care. It is in no way an exhaustive list, but hopefully, may be a useful list in time of need. Additional topics may be found in the topical index.

Answered Prayer
Psalm 3:3-6
Psalm 17:6-8
Psalm 18:1-6
Psalm 37:3-8
Jeremiah 33:3
Matthew 7:7-11
John 15:7-8
John 16:12-13
Romans 8:26-28
1 John 5:13-15

Assurance of salvation
See appendix two

The Blessings of God's Word
Deuteronomy 8:1-10
Psalm 19:7-11
Psalm 119, especially sections such as verses 1-8, 97-105, 165-168
Isaiah 55:10-11
Hebrews 4:11-13
2 Timothy 3:14-16

Comfort

Psalm 23:1-6
Psalm 34:17-19
Isaiah 42:1-42
Isaiah 61:1-3
2 Corinthians 1:3-7
Hebrews 4:14-16

Courage
Deuteronomy 31: 6-8
2 Samuel 10:12
1 Chronicles 22:11-13
2 Chronicles 15:7
Psalm 27:1-5, 13-14
John 16:33

God's presence
Exodus 33:14
Isaiah 41:8-10
Matthew 28:18-20
John 14:16-18
Hebrews 13:5-6

God's Recognition of What You Do
Hebrews 6:9-12
Matthew 10:40-42
Matthew 25:23
Matthew 25:31-40
John 13:12-17
James 1:27

Joy
Psalm 16:5-11
Psalm 30:5
Psalm 100:1-5
Isaiah 51:11
Isaiah 55:12
Zephaniah 3:14-17
Luke 10:18-21

Romans 5:1-5
Philippians 4:4-5
John 15:10-11

Peace
Psalm 4:8
Psalm 46:1-5, 10-11
Psalm 85:8-13
Proverbs 3:1-4
Isaiah 9:6-7
Isaiah 26:3
John 16:26-27
Romans 5:1-5
Philippians 4:6-7
Colossians 3:15-17

Strength/Endurance
Joshua 1:5-10
Psalm 28:6-9
Isaiah 40:27-31
Isaiah 41:8-10
Romans 8:31-39
Ephesians 6:10-18
Philippians 4:10-13
1 Peter 4:12-13

Wisdom/Guidance
Psalm 25:4-10
Psalm 32:8-11
Proverbs 3:5-6
1 Corinthians 2:9-16
James 1:5-8
2 John 1:6

APPENDIX TWO: YOUR RELATIONSHIP WITH CHRIST

This section is offered to help you clarify and maybe gain better understanding of your own spiritual standing with God. Only you know your own heart, and your own relationship with God. Actually, the scripture says that even our hearts can deceive us (see Jeremiah 17:9), so it is important to check our internal senses against the clear teachings of scripture. The first thing I want to encourage you to examine is to recall whether or not you have ever committed your life to Christ. That time is described in many ways, but it is a time when you acknowledge your sin and shortcomings to God, ask His forgiveness and receive adoption into the family of God. Have you experienced that moment in your life? If you don't know for sure, then odds are, you haven't or at least haven't understood when you did and need to clarify for yourself your standing with God.

The scriptures teach that we can KNOW we are securely in God's hand, not merely hope, wish or dream it were so. It is called many things, such as being saved, or born again, but whatever terms you want to use, it is important to know that you belong to and have been accepted by God as His own. One of my favorite passages is 1 John 5:11-13....I strongly encourage you to take time to read it now (there is a table of contents in the front of your Bible....make sure you find 1 John, and not merely John....they are not the same book). For me, this passage makes things pretty clear, as it boils it down to one simple question: do you have the Son of God, or do you not? He is more than willing to partner with you through life, to make you His own dear child, to cleanse you from sin's poison within your soul.

Another helpful scripture is 2 Corinthians 5:21, which you will want to read, but I am going to paraphrase in this way: "For our sake, God somehow made Jesus Christ 'become sin' so that we could become God's righteousness through Christ." A basic outline of what God intends for us can be described as if God offers you and me an exchange, a swap:
> 1) It is not our place to establish the spiritual rules of the universe; we simply learn how God established them from the teachings of scripture. These rules

are real, just as real as gravity that always pulls us toward the earth....we didn't set that one up, either.

2) Sin deserves to be punished (for the wages of sin is death—Romans 6:23). For this discussion, sin can be defined as doing something that is less than God's perfection, or neglecting to do those things God has commanded. In either case, it is simply acting in ways that are not all God designed or desires us to be.

3) Though Jesus did not sin, He suffered punishment by death...which is the penalty for sin, not the penalty for a righteous person like Jesus. So Jesus paid a debt He did not owe and accepted a punishment He did not deserve....He has a credit balance, so to speak.

4) However, you and I *have* sinned. I have yet to meet the perfect person who has never done anything wrong, or always done everything good they could and should. Sometimes we think our sins are smaller than those of others, or not enough to count. When it comes to salvation and entrance to heaven, God doesn't measure our sinfulness by degrees, only in terms of perfect or imperfect (see James 2:10).

5) You and I deserve the punishment of death, because that is the consequence of sin (not merely physical death alone, but death defined as eternal separation from the source of life, separation from God--which is the central concept of hell).

6) Since Jesus didn't sin, He didn't deserve death, He deserved life. It was we who sinned, and we deserve the death. So the deal Jesus offers is this: we can have the life He deserves, if we will trust Him to apply His punishment and death as the substitute penalty owed for our sins.

7) We, however, have to actively accept that offer. A wealthy man can write you a billion dollar check, but it will not make you wealthy until the day you accept it as valid and cash it or deposit it to your own account. Jesus has written you something worth far more than a billion dollars......have you accepted the offer, have you deposited His gift into your life's account? Not sure? Don't know how? Read on.

What we have been discussing is the initial start of the Christian life. It is accomplished, amazingly enough, by simply believing the offer and accepting Jesus' death on the cross as payment for your sin. How? By telling God so! The idea is we trust that God will accept Jesus' sacrifice as an appropriate payment on our behalf, rather than trying to find some other way to pay the penalty myself. Many try other ways such as being good, overcompensating to "make up for" their poor actions, or self-help programs. Strange as it may seem, that is the solution God chose to make available, and since He makes the rules, we should probably use His solution and not try to make up our own, right? Accepting the offer of Christ is accomplished committing your destiny, your forgiveness and your life to Him, trusting He will make His solution work for you. All you have to do is tell God that is what you want, that you want your life to be more pleasing to Him, you want to quit those things that defile you and you want to accept the offer of forgiveness purchased for us through the cross of Christ. But being a Christian isn't merely asking Jesus to come into our hearts and forgive us; it is ALSO committing ourselves to Christ as the ruler and guide of our lives, committing to follow Him and His teachings to the best of our ability. Jesus isn't about handing out tickets to heaven, He is about calling disciples to follow and learn from Him. He is about adopting us into His family, making us His beloved children.

So, what keeps YOU from taking advantage of God's offer for your life? If you haven't already, I invite you to get right with God at this very moment. Below are additional scriptures you can look up to help you better understand these concepts. There is also a short prayer you can use as a guide in your connection with God if you like. But know this: God wants YOU to be part of His family, and to experience the forgiveness He has provided in Jesus Christ. He won't force you to do so, but He invites you to come to Him. *It's okay if you don't understand it all…..the truth is, none of us fully understand all that God has done. But just come to God with what you DO understand, and let that be the beginning you need in this time. God is the one who understands.*

If you do know Christ personally, then I encourage you to examine the depth and commitment of that relationship. Are you following? Will you follow, no matter what, even through this most difficult of experiences? I guarantee you this: if you truly have given your life to Christ, then God's promise and my experience is that you will not have to walk through the tragedy of divorce by yourself…..God Himself will walk with you. And that assurance, at least for me, makes all the difference in the world.

I probably shouldn't leave this topic without pointing out one more thing. Sometimes, people I have dealt with feel unsure about these things. They think that maybe they didn't pray right, or they weren't sure if God answered because they didn't feel what they thought they ought to feel, or they had other ideas and attitudes that create doubt. I want to encourage you to notice that in all the scriptures involved we looked at earlier and below as well, God never says, "maybe." When it comes to God doing His part, He always says that He *will*, He *shall*, it *is*. The scriptures never say of God's promises that He might, it could be, or maybe He will. God can be trusted to follow through on what He has promised. Even if you don't feel like it. Even if you aren't so sure you did everything perfectly. Remember, God knows your heart and your intention, and it is there that He looks. So don't let yourself fret over whether you said exactly the right words to God, or had your eyes closed when you prayed, or whatever. Just have a heart to heart with a God who loves you more than anything, and who will ALWAYS keep His promises for you.

ADDITIONAL SCRIPTURES ON SALVATION

Luke 5:32	2 Corinthians 1:20
Luke 19:10	2 Corinthians 5:14-21
John 3:16-17	Galatians 2:16-20
John 1:12	Ephesians 1:7-8
John 1:1-4, 14	Ephesians 2:8-10
Acts 4:12	2 Thessalonians 1:4-12
Acts 16:31	2 Timothy 2:11-13
Romans 3:10-12, 23	Hebrews 4:12-16
Romans 5:8	1 Peter 1:1-5
Romans 6:23	1 John 5:11-13
Romans 8:26-39	Revelation 3:20
Romans 10:9-10	

SAMPLE PRAYER
God,
    I am looking at my relationship with you, and find that it is not what I want it to be, and that I have not been all you have

wanted me to be. I do believe in your love for me, and your willingness to help me and to save me. I am sorry for all the times I have disappointed you, done things that were wrong when I knew I should have done otherwise. Forgive me for those sins. I want to become your child, and I believe that Jesus' paid the penalty for my sins when He died upon that cross. I come to you to ask you to make me your own, and give me life eternal in your presence. I give my life to you, and will do my best, with your help, to follow you all the days of my life. I love you, God, and appreciate what you have done for me, and look forward to getting to know you better in the years ahead.

In Jesus name, Amen

TOPICAL INDEX (by devotional day)

The following topical index is by no means comprehensive. I have included the major topics for each devotion, though many devotions could fall into multiple categories. The ones listed below are intended simply to help the reader access some material that might be helpful when needed.

INDEX OF SCRIPTURE REFERENCES (by devotional day)

2 Kings 6:15-17 Day 86

6:34 Day 53
10:29-31 Day 96
11:28-30 Day 91
14:15-16 Day 66
17:14-18 Day 7
22:35-40 Day 43
25:14-21 Day 97
25:34-40 Day 67

Mark
5:21-27 Day 49
6:30-32 Day 4

Luke
1:30-32 Day 20
5:17-19 Day 61
12:13-21 Day 46
15:11-32 Days 37 and 38
17:10 Day 99
22:39-46 Day 2

John
3:7-8 Day 8
5:2-9 Day 6
10:27-29 Day 22
11:25-27 Day 93
11:30-36 Day 75
13:5-17 Day 24
14:25-27 Day 9
15:1-5 Day 71
15:12-14 Day 52
19:1-11 Day 28
19:23-27 Day 76
20:11-18 Day 63
21:1-3 Day 100
21:18-22 Day 72

Hebrews
1:13-14 Day 85
2:5-7 Day 85
2:14-16 Day 74
4:8-11 Day 78
4:15-16 Day 3
6:10 Day 99
10:35-37 Day 11
11:8-9 Day 44
13:15 Day 13

James
1:27 Day 68
4:13-14 Day 57

1 Peter
5:7 Day 29

Revelation
5:6-8 Day 77
21:1-4 Day 56

AUTHOR'S BIOGRAPHICAL NOTE
AND CONTACT INFORMATION

Richard Crooks is an ordained American Baptist minister who has been in ministry since 1983, and has served a number of churches and as campus minister in college ministry. He holds Master's degrees from Central Baptist Theological Seminary and Hebrew Union College.

Richard and his wife, Nola, moved to his hometown to offer encouragement and support to his aging parents in their declining years. Daily participation in support and caregiving served as Richard's primary calling during those several years. In the midst of that work, Richard began work on this volume, sharing insights and scriptural reflections out of his own experiences in the ministry of caregiving, as well as from interactions as a pastor for others dealing with a variety of caregiving circumstances. In this process, he became aware of the need for supportive Christian material for individuals serving in this vital role. He has insightful awareness of the dramatic impact caregiving can have on the caregiver, those the caregivers serve, and the various families of those individuals. His own personal struggles and contacts in ministry bring personal impact to these pages. Richard does not claim to have all the answers, nor to have handled all of the issues perfectly himself, but believes it is important to have support, resources and tools from those who have shared the struggle to help loved ones through difficult times in life.

The father of two, he remarried in 2004, and is step father of four children. Previous publications are a two volume set of devotions to help those dealing with the impact of divorce in their lives. The first volume of this set, **Autumn and Winter: Seasons of Loss and Sorrow**, was published in 2012, and the second volume, **Spring and Summer: Seasons of Renewal and Warmth** was published in 2013. The website for Richard's books is findinggoddevotionals.com. You can also contact him through email to seasonsofdivorce@gmail.com or through the findinggodintheseasonsofdivorce facebook page. His writing can be found on www.findinggodintheseasonsofdivorce.blogspot.com.

www.ingramcontent.com/pod-product-compliance
Lightning Source LLC
Chambersburg PA
CBHW032002040426
42448CB00006B/464